Susan Smalley & Stacie Madison : Missing Girls

Pete Dove

Published by Trellis Publishing, 2021.

SUSAN SMALLEY & STACIE MADISON : MISSING GIRLS

First edition. July 12, 2021.

ISBN: 979-8224088799

Written by Pete Dove.

SUSAN SMALLEY & STACIE MADISON : MISSING GIRLS

PETE DOVE

Stacie and Susan – Forever Together

Best friends forever. The bond between teenage girls can be strong. And often is. That was certainly the situation between eighteen-year-old Susan Smalley and her great mate, Stacie Madison, who was just a year younger.

The two were classic late eighties girls. Lots of carefully styled hair, innocent smiles and a love of life. Their bubbly personalities and bright intellects lit up wherever they went.

In the spring of 1988, the two were entering their last few months before graduating from the Newman Smith High School in Carrollton, Texas. Each had their plans and were excited by them. Even though their futures might see them temporarily separated as each pursued their dreams, the fun-loving couple were sure that their friendship would survive any short-term parting.

Susan was already an honour roll student at her school. She was a great ambassador, a young woman who loved meeting new people. She worked as a waitress and planned to develop her burgeoning confidence by moving to the sunny climes of Florida, there to work more widely with people. Her cheerful outlook and sociability made her a popular girl. Her brother, Rich, recalls just how popular his sister had become. 'She was there for her friends at all times,' he said.

Stacie had slightly more orthodox and clearly defined ambitions. For her, college was the route she wished to pursue. She had secured a part time post working for a successful allergist in her hometown and wanted to further her chances of following a career in this important field. Stacie was highly committed to her ambitions, and often had to put social commitments on hold. It was not always easy. With her stunning smile, and classic American good looks – blonde hair and blue eyes to the fore – she had plenty of demands for dates with which to deal.

Her mother recalled how she would tactfully turn down the enquiries of the numerous boys who knocked on her door. 'She was a wonderful daughter,' remembered Ida Madison poignantly.

But on the 19th March 1988 the girls decided that they could enjoy a night out. It was the last day of the spring school vacation, and soon they would be back in classes.

Carrollton is an interesting place. It is frequently identified as one of the best places to live in the US. It is a fair-sized city, with a population of around 120000. But the feel of the city is as though it is much smaller. Perhaps that is down to its earliest days. The community was founded in the middle of the nineteenth century by a number of wealthy landowners, many of whom had originated in another Carrollton – this one in Illinois.

It was, for a third of a century, a wholly agricultural place with the homeliness such an existence brings. That has not changed, although the economic nature of the fledgling city did when the Dallas to Wichita railroad passed through the settlement in 1878. Straight away, Carrollton began to grow. But slowly. Its traditional agricultural heritage was chased, caught and quickly surpassed by industrial developments.

In under ten years the inhabitants swelled from a few homesteads to a permanent population of 150. A school was built, along with two churches and a number of mills and cotton gins. Soon, a second railway criss-crossed the first, and Carrollton expanded further. It became a centre for livestock, cotton and grain. It was the place in Texas that became the logistical heart for the shipping of goods.

But despite this, that small town feel remained. Probably because the population remained relatively tiny. Half a century ago, still just 14000 people lived there.

Then came the surge. In the next decade, numbers rose by nearly 200 per cent. By the time Susan and Stacie went missing, more than 80000 people lived within Carrollton's pleasant boundaries. It is now subsumed into being a suburb of Dallas - a very desirable one, at that – and today its population has grown by another fifty percent.

People from Carrollton are comfortably off. Poverty in the city is rare, and families are often stable. Simply, it is a lovely place to live. There was not the slightest suspicion of the horror that was to unfold on that March night more than thirty years ago.

As we know, Stacie and Susan were sensible girls. Their heads were firmly screwed on. So, their night on the town was carefully planned. Stacie enjoyed ownership of a splendid, daffodil yellow 1967 convertible Mustang (which might have been as much an attraction to the various boys whose tongues lolled out of their mouths at the sight of her as her physical good looks.) The girls set off in the car for an early evening shop at the Prestonwood centre. From there, they ran Susan's mother home from her work at a department store located in the mall.

Carolyn Audett was going out herself that evening, but it did not stop her from reminding the girls to take care of themselves. However, given Carrollton's relative safety, the common sense of the girls and the light evening, she had little worry. Certainly 'not knowing I'd never see them again,' was not a thought which crossed Carolyn's mind. There was no reason why it should.

A friend was holding a party in Arlington, which lies to the west of Dallas. It is a fair drive from Carrollton - to the north west of the city - to the small town, which sits mid-way between Dallas and Fort Worth. But they were teens, and possibly thought nothing of the forty-minute journey they would have to make. So, after changing at Susan's home, they headed off there. The girls stayed at the party for just a short while and left at around 10pm to drive back to Stacie's house. But at midnight, the youngsters did something out of character. Although they had been told to be home by midnight - a reasonable enough expectation for such young adults – they decided to return to the party. It was an odd decision, being so far – close to another ninety minutes of driving there and back, in the dead of night. Still, that is what they appeared to set off to do. Perhaps, though, they changed their mind – or at least had doubts. Because, on the way, they stopped at a Steak and Ale restaurant where Susan worked part time as a waitress.

She chatted to a boy who was a co-worker for a while, and Madison waited in the car. Then the two girls went on their way. As far as is known, their plan was to head back to the party.

Neither girl was seen again.

Susan had been wearing a white sweater set off by blue jeans. She was carrying a blue shoulder bag with a camel coloured trim. Stacie too was wearing a white top, a long-sleeved sweatshirt with a notable pink and orange logo. She was wearing white pants, cotton, and white tennis shoes. Both were dressed to look casual, but smart.

The next morning, Stacie and Susan's panicked parents realised something was wrong. Neither girls' beds had been slept in, and nobody knew where they were. 'I kept pacing and looking out the window, hoping to see her drive up,' remembered Ida.

The parents contacted the police to report their girls missing, and Stacie's easily identified Mustang was soon found. It had been abandoned on a popular strip in the north west of Dallas, Forest Lane. Back in the 1980s this part of the large city was home to movie theatre, popular burger joints and drive through restaurants.

The Mustang contained the girls' jackets, and the doors were locked. It appeared, to all intents and purposes, that the car had been parked normally.

Police in cities such as Dallas are hard pressed. They are used to teenagers behaving badly. Even in such a nice neighbourhood as Carrollton police were familiar with teenagers acting up. And so, as was too often the case in the hard-bitten days at the end of Ronald Reagan's reign, officers from both departments jumped to a conclusion.

Two teenage girls out partying late at night? They had found a couple of boys and were by now shacked up somewhere. Or perhaps, in a fit of teenage pique, they had done a runner. In a short time, like most teenagers, they would be back. As soon as they needed some money, or were hungry, they would come home with their tails between their legs.

Of course, Stacie and Susan's parents knew that their daughters were not like that. They were reliable girls, trustworthy as far as teens can ever be. Nowadays, we know that teenagers' frontal cortexes (a part of the brain) are underdeveloped. It's what makes them so unaware of risk and outright danger. It is probably what led the girls to go out after their curfew in the first place.

It did not make them bad, just normal. But in 1988 people did not have that knowledge of child development; Susan and Stacie were good girls. If their car was abandoned and they were missing, then something bad had happened.

The mismatch in interpretations between parents and the police was great, however. And crucial. Because the police decided that there was no need to search the car in any detail. No requirement to look for fingerprints. No need to search for DNA.

When people go missing, the first twenty-four hours are crucial in finding them safe and well. From today's perspective, the police were negligent in jumping to a conclusion which saw the girls as being at fault for their disappearance. Even back in the days of the late 80s those initial actions ('inactions' might be a better word) of investigators were viewed as dubious.

Some months after Stacie and Susan went missing, the case was handed over to Detective Greg Ward. He was astonished that investigating officers had asked around so little, instead making crucial and very wrong assumptions about what had taken place.

'I'm not saying they screwed up, but they probably could have handled it better,' he said with studied understatement. Detective Ward realised that something sinister had taken place. 'They met someone and got more party than they bargained for,' he observed with a somewhat unwarranted lack of tact.

By this point even the local forces had decided that the girls had not just taken off on their own accord. There was no reason why they should. Nobody else was missing, so they had not run away with some boy or other; both were promising academics with good plans for their futures. They were model students and neither had any troubles of note at school. Both girls got on well with their families. The only plausible conclusion to their disappearance was that they had been abducted. A frightening, but increasingly likely suspicion.

The disappearances cast a giant shadow over the lovely city. 'Anything can happen to anybody,' said Rob Bader, who was a seventeen-year-old junior at Newman Smith High School at the time.

Early clues were thin on the ground. The best seemed to be reports from two witnesses who claimed to see the girls on the night they disappeared. They had been observed hanging around a drag race strip near the LBJ Freeway and Interstate 35E. This was a slightly run-down warehouse district and seemed unlikely to be the kind of place to which the girls would have headed by themselves. Had they met somebody on Forest Road, happily gone with them to the strip in their car, before succumbing to abduction and attack? The probability existed, but despite their investigations, the police could not confirm such a series of events had ensued.

Carrollton police hit dead end after no through road in their failing pursuit of either the girls, or their abductors. At times, their investigation turned to the bizarre. At one point, they contacted a local man called John Catchings. Reasonable enough, we might think. Perhaps he could be a witness, or a man with a lead. Maybe, even, somebody ill informed might presume, he had become a person of interest to the investigation.

Sadly, though, that was not the case. The police contacted, and spent three hours talking to, Catchings because he claimed to be a psychic. In reality, trusting his comments was as likely to be as successful as relying on his observations because his surname – Catchings - might suggest the apprehension of the perpetrators.

Catchings' conclusions were neither particularly surprising nor especially useful. The girls had, he decided, been abducted by a white man aged between 28 and 34 years of age. He wore glasses and had blond hair. This fair-haired homicidal danger had then dumped the girls' body in a local spot called Lake Grapevine. The reservoir was home to, back then, numerous leisurely walks. It was also a popular spot to which teenagers seeking a little illicit peace and quiet would head.

But, it has to be said, their abductor was in all likelihood a man, was probably relatively young and, with two young women in his car, might well head away from the suburbs of Dallas and out into the country where, in the early hours of the morning, he would be likely to find some isolated spot.

In any case, police searched the area before realising that Catchings' reputation may have been a little over blown.

Other tips came to light in the early days of the investigation. These too were less than helpful: a behaviour psychologist reported a 'feeling' that the teens had left the US altogether. He sensed that they had crossed into nearby Mexico in the company of two men. They were allegedly spotted in a Houston supermarket at the same time, more or less, as a caller reported seeing the two youngsters in Bob and Bea's saloon. A not unreasonable claim had Bob and Bea's not been located in Madison, West Virginia. A distance of more than a thousand miles away from their homes. It seems as though the presumably well-meaning caller had been a little mixed up between Stacie's surname and their own hometown.

Another caller offered the remarkably unlikely news that Madison was now in the habit of visiting prisoners incarcerated in a state prison in Florida. Unwilling residents she could not possibly have known. Another caller rang to state 'Susan and Stacie are all right.' This caller then hung up. Police attempted to trace the call, but it had been made from an unrecorded line and was impossible to find.

We have to assume that these hapless and hopeless leads were offered with the best of intentions, if not intelligence, rather than in some attempt to hamper the police's already limited progress. However, we cannot be sure. Whatever the intent, each supposed lead involved a considerable number of wasted police hours. It took officers away from other work – both activities associated with the disappearance of Stacie and Susan, and from other, wider, duties.

Perhaps worst of all, each inaccurate contact raised a spark of hope in the families. A flash that would quickly be extinguished, but which each left a small scar that would never recover; the pit of a cyst long gone but still to be remembered, and agonised over, when that memory was stimulated back to life.

Homicide attracts the most unbalanced members of society – and not just those who actually carry out their deadly crimes.

The lack of progress prayed heavily on the minds of both sets of parents. Stacie Madison's family spent over $3000 on a private detective in a hope that this might throw up a lead. But it did not, and eventually they realised that this drain on their resources was unlikely to ever produce results. Frank, her father, drove around in her classic Mustang. It really was a distinctive car. He lived in the hope that one day a person might see it pass, promoting a memory that would lead to his daughter, and her friend's, discovery. Again, the hope was forlorn.

'It was like they were whisked off the earth,' he said. Still, he continued to drive around until, in 1996, a more physical cancer than the one that was boring away at his heart took hold, and he died. Who can imagine the pain of a father losing their daughter, and then dying without ever discovering what happened to her? Somewhere, out there, resides a killer or killers. Let us hope that they are fully aware of the extended and relentless pain they have caused.

However, despite progressing very slowly, police did have one line of enquiry they decided to pursue. We noted above that the girls had no reason to run away with a boyfriend. But two attractive girls will attract lovers now and then. It is inevitable. In their case, neither Stacie nor Susan had experienced a truly deep relationship with the opposite sex. But Stacie did have someone she might loosely call a boyfriend.

That boy was Kevin Elrod. Their relationship was coming to an end. Stacie found the young lad controlling and overly possessive. Perhaps he could not believe his good fortune in catching such a beautiful girl, perhaps that was just his personality. It cannot be forgotten that Kevin too was still a child in most ways.

On that March day in the spring of 1988, Stacie was determined to end the relationship. But she was not too sure how to do it. It is a sign of her own compassion and mature personality that she did not want to simply ditch her boyfriend, rather to let him down as gently as she could.

'Tell him I'm out with Susan,' was Stacie's instruction to her mum should Kevin ring. He did, and Ida delivered the message. But there was a much stronger reason for the police's interest in the teen. A subsequent girlfriend told the authorities that Kevin had confessed to killing the girls. He said that he had hit them with a shovel and then taken them to a cemetery located close to State Highway 121.

He had buried his victims there, he said. Police swooped. Elrod was taken in for extensive questioning. Police thought that they had their man, despite their negligent actions when they had first found the Mustang.

The boy's story soon began to break down. He was given a polygraph but passed. Then he began to change his story. He had made up his confession, he claimed, because he was sick of people suspecting him. If they are going to blame me anyway, was his juvenile thinking, then I will give them something to blame me for.

Once more, it is worth stating that underdeveloped frontal cortexes lead to problems. In the end, Elrod decided to move away. He also changed his name. It was time to start a new life.

There was a twist to Elrod's tale, however. Many years later he had both married and divorced. His ex-wife then had to have a restraining order placed upon him after he threatened her with a knife. There are many who still suspect that the former boyfriend may have been the murderer of the two girls. However, there is neither circumstantial nor hard evidence to support this. Nothing, in fact, beyond putting together the confession with the later claims of his ex-wife and, most probably, coming up with a conclusion which is not supported by the sum of its two parts.

In 2011 police issued a number of photos which contained images of people they wished to talk to in connection with the likely double homicide. No results were forthcoming.

2013 marked the twenty fifth anniversary of the girls' disappearance. The family held a candle lit vigil with the triple aim of remembering Stacie and Susan, of bringing the now cold case back into the public realm and with the faint hope that memories might be triggered, or long held guilt lead to someone setting the police off in the right direction.

Ida Madison, long widowed, said at the event, 'It horrifies me to think of what probably happened to her. Somebody knows what happened. I think there's somebody out there who knows something.'

She went on to recognise that it was unlikely that either Stacie or Susan were still alive, but still held out the faint hope of getting news. 'I never thought it would be this long,' she said.

A former friend and colleague of Stacie told reporters, 'It's not really an anniversary you want to celebrate, but definitely you want to remember it.'

Blogs and websites spring up around missing persons, especially young ones. These well-meant sites sometimes deliver results and help to keep the missing person somewhat in the public eye. The Deanie Peters Missing Angels blog is one such publication. Set up in response to the case of fourteen-year-old Deanie, who disappeared in 1981 after leaving her middle school, it includes information on Stacie and Susan's case.

The logical conclusion reached is that the girls went with somebody they met and knew. But there was no plan to run away. The blog comes to these observations on the basis that the girls were primarily happy, that there is no evidence they were forced from the car (the hood was up and the car locked) but that the new shoes Stacie had purchased on their shopping trip were still in her bedroom.

It would be very strange to buy new shoes and then run away, leaving them behind. 'I believe they went to Forest Lane wanting to have a fun night, met up with someone they both knew and trusted, got in their vehicle, and left the parking lot,' observed the site. 'What happened next is anybody's guess, but it does not seem good.'

The conclusions of the site seem no less likely to be correct than the observations of police investigators.

According to FBI records, more than half a million people are reported missing every year in the United States. Eighty per cent of them are under the age of twenty-one. In some ways, it is not that unusual that either Stacie or Susan did disappear.

Where their case differs from the norm is in two aspects. Firstly, it is rare for people to disappear together. Where they do, it is usually a couple in love who are looking to set up home somewhere else and start a new life.

Nearly always, in these cases, the lure of home, family and friends eventually becomes too much for one, if not both, of the partners, and they make contact. Secondly, of those five, six, seven hundred thousand people who are reported missing each year, most quickly return of their own accord, and many others are rapidly located. Usually alive, and unhurt. Rarely, but occasionally, some are injured through accident or assault, and even less often it is just their bodies that are found. That must be intensely difficult for family and friends but does allow for some kind of closure to be reached, or at least viewed in the shadowy distance.

But Stacie and Susan have never been found. No trace of them has been discovered. No clue to their disappearance identified. Perhaps the police were not as out of order as it might seem when they consulted a psychic. What else did they have to go on?

A small stone memorial sits in the grounds of the Newman Smith High School. It served as a comfort and a reminder for Ida when she worked at the school for a year after her daughter's disappearance.

But the memory of the girls was already beginning to pass. New youngsters would join the school, those who had been too young to remember anything but a vague anxiousness from their parents when the girls were lost. Many would ask Ida if she knew the girls, making the link between their teacher's surname and the one on the memorial. Few, if any, would consider that their teacher might be Stacie Madison's mom. Teachers do not have personal lives, at least in the eyes of their students.

That grey granite memorial, provided by a local funeral home when it became apparent that the girls were unlikely to return, will be there, it is hoped, long after Stacie and Susan's remaining family pass away. And, probably, long after the killer or killers of these two girls, who had so much in front of them, also passes to wherever he (or she) ends up.

Soon, too soon, the case will fade into oblivion. Maybe, in some future documentary, Stacie and Susan will be remembered. Perhaps even a conclusion might be reached as to what happened to them.

We can take just one tiny piece of comfort: they were best friends. They were out together and, almost certainly, died together. These unfortunate and unsuspecting victims will, we hope, truly remain best friends. Forever.

KILLER MISTRESS: THE TRUE STORY OF TANIA HERMAN

14

LINDA CARLISLE

Tania Lee-Anne Herman, better known in the Australian media as the body-in-the-boot or Mum-in-the-boot killer, was born in Rochester in 1996, just south of the city of Echuca. Echuca is a small town located on the banks of the Murray River and the Campaspe River in Victoria, with its name meaning "Meeting of the Waters" in the local Aboriginal dialect. The town has a population of just over 13 000 and is known as the paddle steamer capital of Australia. Tania was born into a simple, country family. She was the youngest of four children, and she enjoyed a safe and inspiring childhood. Tania was a promising junior swimmer, having won several titles at the state level, and had an incredible flair for the arts. Her lawyer, Julie Sutherland, commented later in her life that Tania "was the embodiment and quintessence of everything noble and decent which one comes to equate with country living, including a strong work ethic and getting on with life despite its vicissitudes." As a high school student, she made money on the side by creating floral bridal hairpieces. None of her friends or family members would have said that Tania was suffering from any difficulties in her younger life, from an early age Tania learned to hide things that were causing her grief. This became something that was characteristic of her throughout her life in an attempt to not cause concern for others.

Before she met "soul mate" Joe Korp who would eventually manipulate Tania into actions that would deprive her of twelve years of freedom, Tania had three significant relationships that left her in a damaged and compromised position. She also endured years of sexual abuse as a child, which she was told was "a special kind of love". When she was older, Tania's first marriage was to John Linton on Sep 26th, 1987 when she was just seventeen. Linton was older than Tania, and their relationship only lasted five months. After this time, Tania met a Columbian student when she was twenty-one and they had a two-year romance. During this time, Tania had her first child, but her partner was cheating on her and Herman eventually found out about the other woman. Her boyfriend left, and later married the woman that he was cheating on Tania with. Finally, in 1996, Tania married Paul Herman who was a charter boat operator in Queensland. Things seemed that they might start to become more stable for Herman. They had Tania's second daughter and moved back to Echuca. However, her husband was a big drinker. Tania reported that her husband would at least go through several slabs and a bottle of bourbon each week and that this began to concern her. However, the real issue for Tania was when Paul became physically violent towards the end of their relationship. In Tania's opinion, this behavior was fueled by his dependency on alcohol and she didn't see a future for them if this continued. Tania left Paul in 2002.

When Tania was 30, she was diagnosed with cervical cancer and had to undergo chemotherapy and radiation therapy for six months. Tania decided not to tell her family about her health issues. When she lost her hair, she claimed that she had shaved it for charity. Tania's desire to keep the troubling news to herself might have made it easier for the manipulative man who was about to arrive on the scene and ask more of Tania than she ever believed she would be capable of doing. After a string of unsuccessful relationships and marriages, Tania, a vulnerable single mother of two, went in search of a new partner online. Unfortunately for her, she stumbled across Joe Korp.

Joe Korp, who was registered on the dating site as Joe Bonte, was posing as a single, self-employed builder. The factory worker was married to Maria Korp, a woman who had immigrated to Australia from Portugal with an earlier, failed marriage. Maria helped to build their house in North Melbourne, being the project bricklayer on the house and directly involved in much of its construction. Unfortunately, almost immediately after they moved in both partners began to express unhappiness in their marriage. Maria had a daughter, Laura, from a previous marriage, and she and Joe had their son Damien together early on in their marriage. When Joe initially connected with Tania in a chat room in October of 2003, he kept his marriage to Maria a secret. There are conflicting claims from different prosecutors as to when Tania became aware of the marriage, some claiming early on and others maintaining that Tania wasn't aware for up to 12 months into their relationship. Whether Tania found out about Maria earlier or later is not of great concern, as this information did nothing to deter her from meeting up with Joe and planning their future life together. During this time, Joe was also seeking out other relationships online, but he provided Tania with a sense of security that he had been searching for her for his whole life. Sources did not report whether or not be actually met up with other women, but the frequency with which he was away from home and the number of times that he was visiting Tania suggest that he had several women. This period may have even been a test for several of these women as to who Joe determined would be capable of killing in the name of their love for him.

The first time that Joe drove to Echuca to meet Tania in February 2004, she showed him the sights around town before having sex in his car down by the Murray River. Joe made many trips like this one over the coming months, hiring cars for the drive and telling Maria that he was in Sydney on business. Joe began to promise Tania the world, even going as far to say that he wanted to buy wedding rings together and have a ceremony in her house as a sort of temporary marriage until they were able to have a real one. Joe promised children to Tania, a long life together, and her much-craved stability. From the moment that she met Joe, Tania began to act as if she was under a spell. Even Tania's lease was registered under the name of Tania Herman Korp. When Paul Herman, one of Tania's previous husbands, had a heart attack while working on a paddleboat, Joe attended the funeral with her. Paul's family later remembered his face when Maria's case was all over the television and newspapers, and some have even wondered whether Pau's death might have occurred under suspicious circumstances. When Joe spoke to Tania, he described his then present marriage as unhappy and sexless, telling Tania how much he was looking forward to the life that they could share together when he was no longer with Maria. Joe assured Tania that the only reason that he hadn't already left Maria was that Maria held incriminating evidence against him and had threatened to take this information to the police if he ever left her. Joe never specified what this information was, holding a lot of things back from Tania. Herman, however, couldn't see this approach.

At this time, Joe became manipulative and domineering. Joe told Tania that he preferred her to only wear black, so those were the clothes that she donned. He told her to distance herself from her friends, so she became isolated. In a prison interview after the death of Maria Korp, Tania divulged information about her mindset at the time. "I think I was sort of brainwashed by him because I was so in love with him and he used to promise me the world — that we'd be married and we'd have a house and we'd have a family and ... it's just one thing after another," she claimed. Eventually, Joe even went so far as to ask her to move closer to him. Tania sold her house and moved to Greendale, by this time acutely aware of Maria and Joe's children. All this time, Joe was finding and meeting up with other women online just as he had done with Tania, but she was unaware of this fact. It is also likely that Joe began to see more of Tania at this time due to her closer location, and that this led to Maria confirming her suspicions that her husband had a mistress. Little did Maria know that events were falling into place that would eventually result in her assault, attempted murder, and death.

In Greendale, Tania enrolled her youngest daughter at the same school as Joe and Maira's son Damien. She even went so far as to list Joe as the emergency contact for her child at the school's office. By this time, Maria was aware that Joe was having an affair. One day, Joe came home to the locks changed and all of his belongings on the lawn. Maria had told friends and relatives about the weekends she spent alone as Joe was on his 'business trips'. During this time, Joe moved in with Tania and he met members of her family, including her brother Stephen Deegan. However, after a brief period, Joe returned to Maria on Christmas Eve. He phoned Tania to assure her that there was still hope for them together, and this is when the pair first began to plot the death of Maria Korp. Tania has stated that the plans began up to a year before the day that she waited for Maria in her garage. During this year, there were a variety of plans including staging a burglary where Joe could bash her to death, and running over Maria with a car. Joe even looked into the cost of hiring a hit man. However, in the end, they settled on Tania taking Maria's life, or what Joe always referred to as "taking care" of his wife, or "getting her out of the road." As the two continued to discuss these ideas, they moved away from a fantasy where they might be able to live together and closer towards practical actions. It is difficult to say whether Joe genuinely wanted to live with Tania and have a future with her. Perhaps if there had been less of an investigation into the matter and he didn't feel the need to incriminate Tania there would have been room for such a life. Either way, at this point, Tanis had no doubts that everything that they were planning was for the future of their love.

During Joe Korps's stay at Tania's house, they discussed how to kill Maria at a pre-Christmas barbecue where her brother Stephen was present. Stephen later contacted the police on the 14th of February regarding the disappearance of Maria Korp, stating that his sister and Joe had talked about several ways of killing Maria in front of Stephen, including using a belt as a ligature. They also asked for Stephen's opinion, saying "What's the best way to knock someone off?" Stephen said that he had encouraged his sister to break off all contact with Joe, and that he "Was crazy and that she should get rid of this guy". As he told police about her reluctance to stop seeing Joe, he noted that it was "Like he had brainwashed her." Stephen also mentioned that in late January Joe was present again and that he and Tania spoke freely in front of Stephen about killing Maria. Furthermore, the night before Maria's disappearance, Tania called Stephen and asked that he visit her as she had something to discuss. During this phone call, Tanis was considerably distressed and going through a moral dilemma. The following is Stephen's account of that discussion as he stated it to the police:

"Tania told me that she and Jo were going to kill Maria. She was very matter of fact about it, and it was like she had already done it. She told me that she was going to use thin cotton gloves, dye her hair, use a swimming cap and black beanie over the top. She also told me what clothes she was going to wear. She said that Jo was going to pick her up and take her to his place. On the way, they would stop and she would get into the boot so that he could smuggle her in. Then she was going to hide behind his car and wait for Maria. She would then sneak up behind her and try to strangle her with a belt. After this, she would put her in the boot of the car and drive the car to the Shrine in Melbourne."

On the morning of the 9th February 2005, Joe Korp drove Tania to his Mount Ridley address at around 6:00AM where she was to lay wait in the garage until Maria came down to drive to work. Joe and Tania had a short conversation in the garage, where he assured her that he loved her. Tania later recounted to police that Joe asked her "How much do you love me? Are you going to show me today?" and also told her that she must make sure that Maria doesn't leave the garage alive. "You've got to get rid of her for me. I want her strangled. I want her dead." Tania had dyed her hair and was wearing the swimming cap, gloves, and black beanie, just as she had told Stephen she would. She hid behind Laura's car and began to rationalize what she was about to do. As she sat there with the strap, and remembers thinking "I shouldn't be doing this. It's not right." Joe had already left for work and the only thing that allowed her to continue the act was repeating Joe's words over and over in her head again that she mustn't let Maria out of the garage alive. In this way, she became somewhat distanced from her actions and it allowed her to go through with the tasks that lay ahead.

When Maria came down the stairs, Tania hooked the strap over Maria's neck and began to apply pressure. Maria screamed and they both tumbled to the ground, Maria fighting for her life and Tania fighting for love. Tania, being physically stronger and larger than Maria, was able to overpower her and won the struggle through sheer force. During these moments, Tania continued to ethically struggle with the actions that saw she herself committing, later saying that "I was in a set frame of mind, but as soon as I saw the blood, something snapped. I panicked," she says. But yet again, by keeping Joe's words in her mind she was able to get through the ordeal. Eventually, Maria slumped down onto the ground and stopped moving. Tania picked her up and dumped Maria in the boot of her own car before taking the keys and preparing to drive to the Shrine of Remembrance in Melbourne. "As I was driving, I couldn't stop crying. I kept thinking, 'This is wrong, this is wrong," Tania claims. On the way, Tania would hear Maria breathing in the boot and came to the realization that she wasn't dead. She heard other sounds as she drove, but didn't know what she could do about the situation. When she got out of the car, the considered other actions that she might take, but settled on leaving Maria in the boot to die. This added another layer to Tania's ethical dilemma, as the death had not been clean cut. For days she would be forced to think about the fact that the woman was still alive in the car, and that every moment that she wasn't going back to retrieve her she was condemning her to death. The only thing that brought her any clarity at this time was the knowledge that now the hardest part was done, and that if they were able to get through the police investigation she and Joe would be able to start the new life that they had spoken so much about. However, Tania was soon to find out that Joe would betray her in his interviews where he would name her as the likely killer.

After parking Maria's car at the Shrine of Remembrance, Tania rushed to Stephen's work on Elizabeth Street in Melbourne at 8:30AM. She asked her brother to drive her to her home in Greenville and seemed calm and collected. Tania told Stephen that she had done as she claimed she would, and killed Maria Korp. Stephen had not previously contacted the police as he didn't believe that his sister would be truly capable of these crimes. Even when she arrived at his workplace and openly confessed, he still didn't believe she had truly done it and took this as one more step to mislead him. Stephen was extremely worried for his sister, and would make fresh attempts to encourage her not to be in contact with Joe, but he was certain that the events that Tania was claiming had passed were either figments of her imagination or attempts at some guise. It wasn't until he saw the news coverage when Maria was found in the boot four days later that he accepted his sister's crimes and called the police to fill in as many details as he could. Tania then met up with Joe and gave over the keys to Maria's car. She told Joe that she was concerned that she hadn't successfully killed Maria, and so that he was "taking a life." Joe allegedly replied: "No, you took the life for me," and soothed Tania, maintaining that she would not be caught. Joe told her to go out into the Lake Eppalock area and burn all of the items that implicated them in the crime. These items included not only the gloves, beanie, swimming cap, and belt that Tania had used at the scene, but also a number of other things that the couple has used as they planned the assault. Other items were also later buried at the Greenvale Reservoir. Later that evening, Joe Korp reported Maria as missing to the Craigieburn Police.

When Joe was interviewed the next morning, the police discussed his relationship with his wife, their financial position, their working commitments, and Joe's connection with Tania Herman. During this interview, Joe was asked if he could think of anybody that would want to hurt Maria, and he immediately told the police that he believed Tania had done it. Joe claimed that Tania wished ill will of Maria and that she was jealous of their marriage. He denied any involvement in the disappearance of his wife, and Joe also claimed that he was slowing down the relationship with Tania. The police then interviewed Herman, who was described as being very cooperative with the police but maintained not only that she hadn't been involved with the crime, but that she had never met Maria and didn't know her. When Tania was released on this day, she attempted to make contact with Joe. She tried to connect with him twenty times through calls and messages, but he didn't respond to any of them. It was around this time that Tania started to wonder whether Joe was planning this all along, and had used her to get out of his marriage with Maria safely and without allegations regarding the sensitive material that his wife had claimed she held. She now began to feel that she had been thrown under the bus, doing Joe's dirty work for him and bound to get stuck with the consequences.

The search for Maria Korp continued for four long days until a gardener recognized her car from the news bulletins. Those who opened the boot claim that they thought Maria was already dead due to the stench and the state of her body. When they realized that she was breathing, Maria was rushed to the Alfred Hospital and put into intensive care. The initial diagnosis was that she had suffered from strangulation, dehydration, and prolonged loss of consciousness, which had resulted in brain injury. Later on that day, Maria was examined by Forensic Physician Dr. Morris Odell, who categorized which injuries were a result of the initial struggle and which were a result of her incarceration in the boot of the car. Odell noted that her neck injuries were likely caused by the application of a ligature. Maria stayed in a coma, and she was fed intravenously before being moved onto nasogastric feeding before percutaneous entrogastric tube feeding. The doctors monitored her neurological state with MRIs, which showed a progressive loss of brain substance which suggested that her initial diagnosis of having a severe hypoxic brain injury was accurate. When Maria did not improve over months, the decision was made on the 27th July to cease her medical management and tube feeding as her condition was perceived to be terminal. At fifty years old, Maria Korp died in Alfred Hospital at 2:40AM on the 5th August 2005.

On the afternoon of the 16th February 2005, both Joe and Tania were interviewed once more. For the third time, Joe was interviewed and maintained his stance that he had nothing to do with the attempted murder of his wife. Joe made no comment on the questions that were asked of him, and Tania Herman made full admissions to not only her involvement in the attempted murder but details about Joe being her accomplice. By this time, Tania had realized Joe's intentions to pin the entire event on her and had begun to wake up from her spellbound period of infatuation with him. Even though she still loved Joe dearly, she felt that the truth about the situation had to be told. Tanis was charged with attempted murder. On the 1st July 2005, Tania was charged with twelve years imprisonment with a non-parole time of nine years. Joe Korp, who was charged and remanded in custody, had been released on the 9th June to stand before the Supreme Court on the 3rd August. Joe wrote a letter to Tania, which he had his sister deliver. In this, he insisted that there was still a chance for them if she wanted it. "I think I was sort of brainwashed by him because I was so in love with him and he used to promise me the world — that we'd be married and we'd have a house and we'd have a family and ... it's just one thing after another," Tania claimed. Over the years to come, through the counseling that she would receive in the prison system and the friends that she would make there, Tania would come to understand that way that Joe treated her. These new perspectives would give her a whole new outlook on these years of her life and the ways in which he was treating her.

On the day of Maria's funeral, Joe went out into the shed of the house that he shared with Maria. He wrote a series of diary entries, notes, and letters, and stuck up pictures of Maria on the shed walls. Joe hung himself, and one of the notes which were left close to where he was found hanging read "F-ck all those who thought I was guilty" and "Where's the justice...no f———evidence." In all of these letters and diary entries, he maintained his innocence and his love for Maria. In one letter to a daughter of his, Mia, from a previous marriage, he wrote:

"Mia, Oh my only daughter.

"I have loved you and cried for you all my life.

"It was nice to see you and become close again.

"Please forgive me for leaving you again.

"Please understand about love.

"I found it and lost it with Maria.

"Stupid me."

At this time, Herman was devastated. In one session with the prison counselor, she revealed: "If he's not alive I don't want to live." Tania went into a long period of silence after this, resistant to talking about the case with anybody who came by to interview her. Eventually, she opened up to one writer, Rochelle Jackson, who was putting together a collection called Partners in Crime: The true stories of eight women and their lives with notorious men which were published in 2012 by Allen and Unwin. It is from these interviews that we have come to understand so much more about Tania and the experiences that she went through. It is also due to this text that we can gain some insight into how she was reflecting on her actions and her time with Joe. During this interview, Tania expressed to the world that her biggest regret was taking a mother away from her children, eleven-year-old Damien and twenty-seven year old Laura. Tania, a mother herself, found herself haunted by this fact and named this as the place where she harbored the most guilt regarding the whole series of events. Tania only had sporadic contact with her own daughters during her jail sentence. Eventually, Tania began to show signs of accepting the things that she had done and wanting to grow past them: "I've done his crime and now I'm doing his time. The past is the past and I can't undo it — I just have to move on."

Tania was initially incarcerated in the Dame Phyllis Frost maximum security prison. It is Victoria's largest women's prison, holding 260 prisoners, and dedicated to the philanthropist Dame Phyllis Frost, who was particularly concerned with the welfare of female prisoners. Aside from Prison Tarrengower which is a minimum security prison, which Tania was later transferred to, The Dame Phyllis Frost Centre is the only women's prison in Victoria. Aside from Tania Herman, there are several other prisoners who have spent time at the center that have captured Australian headlines. Vicky Roach, an indigenous activist, fought the High Court while in jail in a case that overturned an attempt to remove the vote from serving prisoners. Andrea Mohr, a German writer, served time for international drug smuggling and organized crime. Wendy Peirce, Roberta Williams, and Renate Mokbel were also inmates of the facility, both being figures in the Melbourne underworld as represented in the popular Underbelly series. However, probably the most famous inmate is Judy Moran who was the queen of the Melbourne underworld, murdering her brother-in-law Des "Tuppence" Moran. There are rumors that Herman and Moran had an altercation one day in the prison, but these allegations were denied by prison staff. The claim was that Herman had won a turf-war in the prison, with Moran having previously been the top dog. In the center, Herman was known as Muscles. Some sources claim that Tania punched Moran, and others claim that this turf-war was won purely on words. Tania was eventually moved from the maximum security prison to Tarrengower, where she began to pick up the pieces of her life.

Tarrengower held a lot of opportunities for Tania. During this time she began a degree in fine arts, took an interest in cooking, dressed up as Santa for the Christmas celebrations, and developed a friendship with her cellmate Bernadette Denny. Denny was in the system for the Herman Rockefeller murder which had occurred in January of 2010. Denny, an alcoholic pensioner, and her partner Mario Schembri, a sheet metal worker, got into contact with millionaire Rockefeller through an advertisement for couple swinging in a local newspaper.

Herman claimed that he and his wife were interested in swinging together, but when he arrived he was alone, his wife knew nothing of the matter. Herman engaged in intercourse with Denny while Schembri watched, and promised to bring his wife the next time that he arrived. When he arrived frazzled one evening demanding sex of Denny with no wife in sight, the couple became aggressive. Rockefeller kept attempting to grab and sexually assault Denny, So Schembri and Rockefeller became involved in a brawl which Denny joined. This interaction became more and more violent until Rockefeller apparently fell over and knocked his dead, causing his death. After this, the couple went shopping for materials to dispose of the body, being seen on a hardware store camera buying plastic drop sheets and testing the weight of a chainsaw. They dismembered his body and Schembri took the remains to a friend's house where he burnt the parts over time. Tania became very close to Denny, and publically defended her as a good woman. During this time, Tania also met her current lover Nicky Muscat.

Nicky Muscat was in Tarrengower as a fraudster, having stolen $118 000 from the pokies venue that he had managed. During their time at Tarrengower, a relationship developed between Nicky and Tania and they even asked for a ceremony where they could be married behind bars. This event became highly publicized in the Australian media and brought a lot of attention back to the case. This request was denied, but their love stayed strong. On the 14th February 2014, Tania Herman was released from prison. Nicky, who had been released from the prison the year earlier, arrived to pick her up in a silver 4WD and took her to her home in Yarraville. Over the next few days, the couple was spotted walking around their local streets and stores hand-in-hand, with Tania beginning to pick up the pieces. Tania and Nicky are still together, adjusting to life on the outside and trying to make up for the time that they each lost in prison. Perhaps they offer each other an understanding that many people would not be capable of. Finally,

Tania has found a relationship with the stability, respect, and understanding that she has always been looking for.

GIRL STRANGLER:

THE TRUE STORY OF SERIAL KILLER DANA SUE GRAY

ERIN PIERCE

Dana Sue Gray was born on December 6th, 1957 in Pasadena, California. Her mother, Beverly Arnett, was a former beauty queen who worked as a professional model. Her father, Russell Armbrust, worked as a hairdresser and was married three times prior to marrying Beverly. The couple had several miscarriages before Dana was born.

Her mother was born for the camera and loved attention. She liked being pampered, getting her make-up done and wearing flashy outfits. Beverly modeled for Bullock's, did print ads for Hamilton watches and was once a Rose Princess at the Tournament of Roses Parade.

LIKE MOTHER LIKE DAUGHTER

Russell divorced Beverly, however, when he witnessed his wife attack an older woman that had angered her. Beverly had also maxed out his credit cards, putting him financial peril. Dana was only two years old at the time of the divorce and rarely saw her father.

"Some kind of estrangement had taken place," forensic psychologist Lora Dixon said. "After her parents divorced she had turned down invitations in her teen years to visit her father on all of the holidays and birthday get-togethers."

"There is also something to think about here in terms of Beverly's own temper. Dana clearly witnessed violence and bullying from her mother at an early age. She inherited those characteristics from her mother with tragic results."

Dana had discipline problems early on as she sought attention from her narcissistic mother. Her mother would discipline her but Dana would retaliate by stealing money to buy candy. Her mother had two other children from a previous marriage. Dana would go into the rooms of her step brothers and urinate in their beds.

Her mother would continue to try and discipline her to no avail as Dana would lash back with violence. This facet of her personality was never placed under her control.

"Mommy and daughter didn't get along," Dixon said. "But obviously that isn't unusual nor does mean she was destined to become a serial killer. There was some deep seated issues festering here though. This is evident when Dana gave her mother a snake for Christmas. 'A snake for a snake' the card must have read."

Nonetheless, it did not appear on the surface that Dana had to endure the brutal childhood that gave birth to so many other serial killers. Cedric Ward, one of her step brothers, did admit that Dana did not have the best of childhoods. "It was not happy growing up," he recalled.

SCHOOL AND SEX

Dana did not get along with other students and achieved low grades in all of her classes. She was a chronic truancy case and often forged notes to get out of class. Dara was sexually active at a very early age as she would lose her virginity at the age of twelve. She would ultimately go from one relationship to the next, using sex to lure men into her web of narcissism.

"Dana has a problem," said Richard Singer, a boyfriend of her mother. "She does not want to be told no. She has her own thing, and nobody could tell her any different. You could not tell Dana what to do."

"Her mother would pretty much try to control her, but Dana would go off on you. You could not tell her what to do. Dana is very hyperactive and opinionated."

During her adolescent years, she loved horror movies and read Grimm's Fairy Tales numerous times. As a teenager, she and a neighbor built a catapult. They would tie tiny parachutes on the cat's backs and then hurl them into the air, with the parachute carrying them down into neighborhood swimming pools.

A MOTHER'S DEATH

Beverly contracted breast cancer when Dana was fourteen. Dana decided to become a nurse after witnessing the way the nurses at the hospital treated her mother. Her mother died and Dana was forced back to live with her father.

"The temptation here is to say that Dana was inspired to become a nurse by witnessing the compassion the nurses shown her mother during her illness," Dixon said. "But I would posit a different psychological scenario. Dana saw that the nurses had power over her mother. That for once, her mother was weak and had to defer to other people for the first time in her life. Dana wanted power. Control. What better way to get that then to become a nurse?"

Dana went into a depression after her mother died and would reveal her sentimentality in letters she would write to her then boyfriend, Don Lane, in jail.

"Tomorrow, Good Friday, 4-1-94, is also April Fool's and also my real mom's 76th B-day. It's been 22 years since her death, and I still celebrate her B-day for her. I celebrate it for her 'cause she died when I was 14 and we never got to get past the 'grow years' to become friends like my dad and I are. She was wild-but made my younger years a total adventure: camping, clamming @ Pismo, best Halloween parties and the best Xmases a poor family could have. She could make a fun time out of just anything."

"Again, you see in her letters a sense of victimhood," Dixon said. "She makes no mention of her mother ignoring her birthdays. And she describes her family as 'poor.' They lived in relatively affluent area, becoming strapped for cash primarily because of Beverly's spending."

GROWING UP

Dana's father Russell had remarried, living with his new wife Yvonne who had a daughter named Cathy. Dana would move in with the couple, sharing a room with Cathy. The reunion between her and her father would be a short-lived one, however, as Yvonne would find marijuana in Dana's room.

Russell's wife then kicked Dana out of the home.

On her own at the age of fifteen, Dana would move-in with her sky-diving instructor, Rob Beaudry. The union would produce two pregnancies but Rob talked Dana in to getting abortions both times. These were decisions that she would later come to resent.

At five-foot-two and weighing a stocky 135 lbs, Dana would nonetheless inherit her mother's penchant for fancy clothes and desire to be pampered with manicures and pedicures. Despite her taste in high-end living, associates would describe her appearance and demeanor as "hard."

She would graduate from Newport High School in 1976 and enter nursing school at Saddleback College in Mission Viejo, California. Dana paid her way through nursing school while working as waitress. She also taught herself screen printing techniques and sold screen printed items for extra cash.

"Dana inherited her mother's psychology when it came to money and relationships," Dixon said. "She operated from a 'lack mindset', in that she always saw herself as poor. She was industrious but felt sorry for herself that she had to work so hard, paying her way through school and working for a living. The shopping sprees were a relief to her perceived burden."

ESTRANGED FROM FAMILY

Dana became estranged from her half-brothers, her older siblings from Beverly's previous marriage. The reasons were always financial as she become embroiled in a dispute over the proceedings from their aunt's estate.

She had run-ins with her half-brother Rick in particular.

Dana reacted with anger after he told her to sell belongings to pay her mounting bills. Rick wrote back telling her that she had no consideration for others.

"Nuts," is how her sister-in-law described her. "Not even normally greedy. Crazy. Gray is missing a conscience. I do not think it is there. When you talk to her, she has no concept of other human beings."

"The half-brothers clearly knew she was trouble," Dixon said. "They did the right thing in distancing themselves.

NURSING CAREER.

Immediately upon graduating from Saddleback, Dana landed a nursing job at Corona Community Hospital. She used that as a springboard to a high paying position as an operating room nurse at Inland Valley Regional Medical Center (some reports have her identified as a labor and delivery nurse). She was described by one nursing supervisor as "very caring."

During this time, she had found another boyfriend, a windsurfer whom she would accompany on trips to Hawaii where they would pursue various outdoor activities. This relationship would be an on-again, off-again type deal until Dana would marry Tom Gray. The couple would tie the knot at a winery in the affluent Temecula area.

Tom was an active sportsman and had a crush on Dana since high school.

"She was a hard core athlete," Tom recalled. "A sky diver, wind surfer, mountain bike enthusiast and snorkeler, and she was skilled in each sport."

Dana took pride in her physical strength and would often roll up her sleeve to reveal her bicep muscle. 'She how strong I am?' she would ask.

Living in the gated community of the affluent Canyon Lake suited Dana as it would have been something that would have pleased her mother. Her and Tom started numerous businesses where they used the name "Graymatter."

Tom could not stop Dana's spending habits, however. The couple took out a loan for $47,000 and another for $20,000 within the first nine months of their marriage.

"She was replicating the marriage of her mother and father," Dixon said. "She liked the empowerment that came from having a lot of money. Having money, or rather the act of spending money is what fed her ego. Only in Dana's case she took it way beyond her mother. She was willing to kill for that feeling."

The marriage quickly soured when Dana's spending habits sent the couple into overwhelming consumer debt. Her alcoholism also worsened, particularly after she suffered a miscarriage. Dana indulged in three or four glasses of wine while cooking dinner and then having more with the dinner itself. Her days off from the hospital were adventures in bourbon whiskey, 7-Up and Tequila shooters. Later, she would admit to using marijuana and cocaine.

When Gray unexpectedly received a $7500 inheritance, Dana took the money and blew it on a trip to Europe, leaving her husband behind at home. When she returned , she began an affair with Don Lane, a musician in her husband's band. When Lane agreed to support her, she moved out of the Canyon Lake house and spent $11,000 in five months.

In March of 1992, however, Dana began seeing a psychiatrist. He prescribed Paxil for her, probably to stave off depression among other things.

Lane had a five year old son at the time and would later tell authorities of Dana's "mood changes" and her propensity to break out into "hysterical tears" with little provocation.

She filed for divorce from Tom but this would not be finalized until much later. In September of 1993, Tom and Dana were forced to file for bankruptcy to prevent foreclosure on their Canyon Lake residence.

Despite the value of the home increasing, the amount they owed on the house was more than its worth. They owed $177,500 on a house valued at $125,000 because of double mortgages.

She suffered a miscarriage, exacerbating more depression as well as alcohol and drug abuse.

FIRED FROM THE HOSPITAL

The trouble continued for Dana as two months later she would be fired from the hospital for stealing Demerol and other opiate pain killers.

"What Dana was trying to do was medicate herself," Dixon said. "The new marriage, the exotic vacations, the fancy house and cars. It was never enough to quell the demons that spoke in her head. A control freak out of control. So she struggled to constantly fill the void with booze and drugs. Then this spirals into an affair with a friend of her husband. Again, this life trajectory happens to a lot of people. In Dana's case, however, she needed that extra thrill. Something more than the rush of sky-diving, cheating on her husband, and getting high. She needed the ultimate adrenaline rush. The power to take someone's life."

TIME TO KILL

In later reports, hospital authorities would reveal their own problems with Gray.

"She is sarcastic," Darlena Addison, the former nursing supervisor who fired Gray for stealing drugs. "She does get her point across if she's crossed or doesn't get her way."

"The problem was a condescending attitude, as Dana believed that she was smarter than everyone and had a need to dominate."

The hospital would later report that they did not have any "unusual" deaths during Gray's tenure.

"Of course that is what you would expect them to say," Dixon said. "If they admit to any 'unusual' deaths then it certainly opens them up to a lawsuit. The opportunity would certainly be there for Dana to steal credit cards from elderly patients and rack up bills. It appears, however, that she did not put her murderous impulses into action until after her dismissal. Dana fell in love with the struggle. The fight of her victim as long as she would emerge on he winning end. Poisoning her victims to death in the way it would have been possible for her as a nurse would not have given her that adrenaline rush."

After the loss of her job, Dana would amp up her indulgences in alcohol, drinking straight Vodka, loving the Smirnoff brand in particular.

On Valentine's Day in 1994, Dana contacted Tom's parents (after their separation he had kept his phone number and address a secret). She informed Tom's parents that she wanted to meet with him.

Tom agreed at first but later did not show up.

Tom would find out that Dana had taken out an insurance policy on him without his knowledge. The policy payout would have been enough to pay down the Canyon Lake home the couple used to share.

Later that day, Dana murdered Norma Davis.

THE FIRST VICTIM

Norma Davis was 86 years old at the time. She was the mother-in-law of the woman (Jeri Davis Armbrust) who married Dana's father in 1988. Jeri's first husband, Bill Davis, was Norma's son. Bill died in the early 1980s, and his widow married a newly divorced Russell.

But Jeri continued to care for her elderly mother-in-law, even after she remarried. Dana would also come to know Norma very well.

On February 16th, 1994, however, the body of Norma Davis would be found by a neighbor named Alice Williams. She had been dead for two days as someone had stabbed her in the neck with a wood-handled utility knife. The blade had been inserted so deep that it nearly severed Norma's head.

She also had a filet knife sticking out of her chest.

Police would discover no forced entry into the home. Norma always kept the doors locked unless she was expecting a visitor. Her neighbor, Alice, stated that she could not remember if Norma had mentioned she was expecting company.

"We didn't have a lot of information," Detective Joe Greco said. "The only piece of evidence that we had was the entry way of the condominium. There was a faint shoe print on the condominium and it was a 6 ½ size shoe."

Detectives would find the Nike shoe print and Davis' Social Security check in plain view. Additionally, on the first floor of the condo, they found a smear of blood on an armchair and a torn phone cord.

A modus operandi had been established. Dana would manually strangle her victims with a phone cord, then use an object to smash or stab.

The coroner concluded that Norma Davis was strangled first then stabbed. She was stabbed eleven times with Dana leaving the knives stuck in her body.

Police described the scene as one of the most brutal they had ever encountered.

"It was a shock because it was only my second homicide case as a detective," Greco said. "It was overwhelming. It crossed my mind that I had a serial killer on my hands."

SHE DEVIL ON A RAMPAGE

"The community was very affluent," Greco said. "They don't have a lot of homicides."

On February 28th, 1994, 66-year old June Roberts was found murdered. She had lived in the gated community of Canyon Lake along with Dana.

Dana had known Roberts and visited her that day saying that she wanted to borrow a book about either overcoming alcohol addiction or vitamins, the reports vary. Dana had her boyfriend's five year old son waiting out in front in her Cadillac.

Ignorant of Dana's true motives, Roberts allowed Dana into her home. She went to retrieve the book Dana inquired about while her would-be killer ripped out the cords to June's phone

Dana would later describe their interaction taking a turn when she became "really annoyed" that June came back with the wrong book. She also told a psychologist that she became infuriated that June allegedly said that she "didn't do enough" to save her marriage with Tom.

When asked what made Dana believe that Roberts and her other victims were looking down on her, Dana responded that she did not like their body language.

"The arching of the eyebrow," Dana said. "That is what happened. All three."

Dana then used the phone cord to strangle Roberts to death.

"I was right behind her," Dana recalled. "I choked her with the phone cord. She was holding on, trying to get the cord off. I pulled her down. She was on her back. I hit her in the head with a bottle. I lost it. I was so consumed. I don't know the time span in there-must have been very quick. She must have stopped moving, and I left. As I walked out, she had a little wallet thing. I grabbed it."

"We went out and proceeded to shop up a storm. "

In talking to psychologists,.Dana appeared unaware of the concept of remorse.

"It was very brutal," Greco said. "The victim had been strangled with her own telephone cord and actually tied to a chair. And she was struck so hard (by the wine bottle) she fractured her skull."

Her autopsy noted a "moderately deep ligature furrow" and a "6 x 3 purple contusion." The cranium contusion was caused by a heavy glass wine bottle striking her with tremendous force. The volume of blood in and near the bathroom door, the walls and pooling under the body made it impossible to gauge the age of the victim.

"This is when the profile of Dana Sue becomes highly unusual," Dixon said. "With female serial killers, you usually see poison or the use of a gun as the weapon of choice. Dana Sue, however, approached her victims with a high level of physical violence that rivaled a male serial killer. There was nothing lady-like about her approach. She was a cold blooded, hands on killer."

TIME TO SHOP

Dana did not hesitate after murdering Roberts, she had to get her shopping fix met.

She would go to Bally's Wine Country Cafe in Temecula, eat crab cake and scampi while charging the meal to Robert's credit card. She could not finish the entire meal, however, and had the waitress pack the rest.

She then got an eyebrow wax and a perm then treated her boyfriend's son to a stylish haircut.

"The fact that she had the little boy accompany her on both the murders and the shopping trips deserves mention," Dixon said. "Dana remained childless throughout life. She was regretted getting two abortions and suffered a miscarriage during her marriage with Tom. Going out and about with her boyfriend's son made her feel like a Mommy. She could be the Mommy that she never had, treating the young child to things she always wanted."

Dana signed "June Roberts" on the $164.76 charge at the salon. She then went to the mall and spent $511 on a black suede jacket, several pairs of cowboy boots, and then $161 on a pair of diamond earrings all charged to Roberts. Her addiction still not satiated, she went to a drug store, picking up dog treats, two bottles of Smirnoff and a toy police helicopter for the boy.

The day after, Dana loaded up on suntan lotion, got a massage at Murrieta Hot Springs resort and then went on another power shopping spree.

"She had absolutely no remorse," Dixon said. "There was no hiding out and laying low like some other wimpy male serial killer. Dana Sue was different. She killed and then she had to do the one thing that gratified her. She had to get to the mall. She had to get the high from buying stuff. She had to enjoy the power while it still lasted."

Ironically, none of her victims had anything stolen aside from their credit cards.

"Dana didn't take any rings from her victims," Greco said. "Or some valuables from the home that were obvious. So I don't think any of the crimes were motivated by money."

Ten days after the Roberts' murder, Dana would enter an antique store, the Main Street Trading Post in Lake Elsinore. Dana stated to the cashier, Dorinda Hawkins, that she wanted to buy a picture frame for a photo of her deceased mother.

"Dana came in asking about picture frames," Greco said. "During their interaction, Dana felt that Dorinda was being condescending to her.

"I felt sick to my stomach," Dana said. "I wanted to vomit. I wanted her to die."

Dana asked if Hawkins was working alone and then she attacked her, strangling her with the store's telephone cord.

"Dorinda is begging for her life when Dana is strangling her," Greco said. "And Dorinda told her 'you can have anything you want. Take the cash, I have eight kids, just let me live.' And Dana told her 'I'm not doing this for the money.' She said that twice. And that really gives you an insight on what Dana is thinking while she's committing these crimes."

Dorinda, however, continued to fight, resisting Dana all the way.

"Relax," Dana said, trying to coax Hawkins into dying. "Just relax."

Hawkins grabbed a broom and poked Dana with it to no avail.

Dana then shoved Hawkins to the ground and stepped on her head as a brace to better choke her.

"Her eyes were flat," Hawkins recalled. "I could tell she had killed before."

Believing her victim dead, Dana stole five dollars from Hawkins' purse and twenty dollars from the cash register.

An hour later, she began another shopping spree, still using Roberts' credit cards.

Hawkins, however, would survive the attack and provide the police the required description of Dana.

THE ATTACKS CONTINUE

Nearly a month after her first killing, on March 16th, 1994, Dana would kill the 87-year old Dora Beebe.

Moments after Beebe arrived home from a doctor's appointment, Dana pulled up in front of her house. She knocked on the door and asked Beebe for directions.

"Here we see Dana getting bolder," Dixon said. "With Norma Davis and June Roberts, she knew the victims beforehand. And the attempted murder in the antique store seemed to be a spur of the moment thing. But the Beebe murder is the first occasion where Dana has picked out a stranger. Elderly women were her preferred target, specifically those who were alone, and tragically Beebe emerged in her cross-hairs."

Living in the same neighborhood for several years, it was improbable for Dana to become lost. But she used that as an excuse when she came knocking on Beebe's door asking for directions.

Dana became angry when Beebe said "I don't have time for this." She was able to hide her anger as Beebe capitulated and allowed Dana insider her home to look at a map. Once inside the home, however, Dana assaulted the elderly woman.

'She turned her back on me," Dana said. "I choked her with the phone cord. I hit her in the head with an iron. As I remember it, it wasn't much of a fight."

Using a stainless steel Black and Decker iron that Dana found in the home, Dana bashed Beebe in the head so hard that it dented the appliance.

Less then an hour later, Dana would be at the mall with Beebe's credit cards in hand.

"She enjoyed doing things that were risky," Greco said. "She was a thrill seeker. I think that she really enjoyed what she was doing. She got a thrill out of it."

PANIC IN THE STREETS

The residents in the gated community of Canyon Lake went into panic mode. Some of the elderly citizens moved in with family until the killer was caught. A group of elderly widows organized themselves to sleep together at designated houses, not wanting to be alone.

There were some who thought the killings where the product of a cult engaging in the ritual sacrifice of the elderly.

"Rumors circulated around the entire community," Dixon said. "A terrifying time for everyone, the elderly in particular. This was a relatively well-to-do neighborhood. People were unused to killings, let alone a serial killer. Numerous people bought guns and kept it by their bedside while others banded together in the belief that there were safety in numbers."

FALSE SUSPECT

Police detectives were at a loss early on in finding a suspect. Prospects were so bleak that a supervisor in charge had seriously thought about using a psychic. Dana was not anywhere near the police's list of possible killers. Instead, the police initially suspected that her mother-in-law, Jeri Armbrust, might be the killer.

The police determined that Armbrust used to be married to Davis' son and continued to care for her former mother-in-law.

Detectives grew suspicious because it was unusual that Jeri would continue to take care of someone who was not a blood relative. Norma Davis herself was on death's door, recovering from a triple bypass surgery.

Police determined that Jeri had been in Davis' house the Sunday before the murder and that she wore a pair of Nike shoes.

Jeri stated that she did come to Davis' house but only came to drop off groceries. She heard the TV on upstairs but did not go up to say hello. She left the groceries on the counter and went home.

Police questioned why she didn't say hello but after weeks of questioning police determined that Jeri was not a suspect. She instead became an ally to the investigation.

CAPTURE

Descriptions obtained from the various merchants at the shopping center were eventually used to catch Dana. She had been buying so much stuff that the credit card company called June Roberts' family to inquire about the excessive spending.

Police detectives went to all of the stores where Roberts' credit card had been used, interviewing the cashiers. They obtained a physical description of Dana, surmising that the killer had dyed her hair recently and was accompanied by a little boy.

Detective Greco relayed this information to Jeri Armbrust.

Jeri surmised that the killer was in fact, her step-daughter Dana. She said that Dana recently dyed her hair red and had a boyfriend who had a young son.

Greco then obtained a search warrant and called for the aid of ARCNET (Allied Riverside County Narcotics Enforcement Team) to stake out Gray's home in Lake Elsinore.

Unfortunately, Dana was murdering Dora Beebe just hours before they determined her to be the killer. They followed Dana to a bank where she used Beebe's credit card and then went out for another shopping spree.

"We were able to follow the paper trail created by the use of these credit cards," Greco said. "With the merchants we were able to get a general description of the suspect."

Later that day, Greco arrested Dana while she was cooking dinner. Assisting officers took her boyfriend and his son in for questioning.

HOUSE OF STOLEN GOODS

Police did a thorough search of Dana's home after her arrest.

"They found jewelry, food, liquor, a ski mask, a purse with nearly $2,000 stuck in the washing machine, and many items of clothing," one report stated. "The police obtained a wealth of evidence: Gray's use of credit cards, clerks who had seen her directly after each murder, handwriting experts who identified her signatures on various items."

Dana was interrogated for hours.

"In the interview," Greco recalled. "Dana talked about finding a purse. And that purse belonged to a woman by the name of Dora Beebe. I knew that I had the right suspect in this case. But I didn't not know that on the same day we were serving her search warrant she was killing her last victim."

Dana stated that she never took the credit cards but after police revealed that they had evidence of her using them, Dana claimed that she found both Roberts' and Beebe's cards.

She maintained this story throughout the questioning. When asked why she kept the cards she said that she "had an overwhelming need to shop."

NO REMORSE, NO SYMPATHY

Dana displayed no sympathy for the victims. One psychologist noted that some of Dana's answers were like a robot answering in a manner they believed a normal human should.

After a hearing, Deputy District Attorney Richard Bentley wanted the death penalty. Dana pleaded insanity for all charges. But a witness came forward and stated that she saw Dana at Roberts' house on the day of her death, Dana quickly changed her plea to guilty and robbing and murdering two women as well as the attempted murder at the antique shop.

"At the end of the day," Dixon said. "Dana didn't want to die. When a witness came forward and said she saw Dana at the Roberts' house perhaps she knew that she was done for and would have been executed. Maybe she did not have enough confidence in her ability to pull off the insanity defense. So she struck a deal. She would plead guilty and avoid the death penalty."

Nonetheless, prosecutors were still unable to determine how Dana left the bloody crime scenes without a speck of blood on her or any sign of a struggle. All the clerks and waitresses spotted nothing out of the usual.

LIFE WITHOUT PAROLE

On October 16th, 1998, Dana Sue Gray was sentenced to life without parole.

"It's hard to find words to describe the atrocity in this case," Judge Patrick Magers said during Dana's sentencing. "The crimes were horrendous, callous and despicable."

Dana is currently jailed at the California Women's Prison in Chowchilla.

"She enjoyed the power," Dixon said. "She got addicted to the power she obtained while she killed people who were helpless to fight back. She liked watching them struggle. Liked having control over them before they died."

Jail has not seemed to bother Dana as she referred to her incarceration as her "county condo." She continues to pester her jailers to replicate her high-maintenance civilian lifestyle. She insists on a vegetarian diet and wants the use of a chiropractor. She has requested a mirror and has lobbied consistently for the return of her belongings.

Dana has drawn chilling clown faces, cobbling her paints together from M&M's candy coating, cherry drink mix, lipstick and and baby powder.

Her family came to visit her and brought her a pair of cheap Nike's. She refused them, wanting the high-end models.

Dana continues to thumb her nose at authorities as she sometimes sends collectibles to "murderablia" websites. She has sold her panties at $250, where she autographs them and writes in her prison identification number. She sells her hand tracing for $65 and a 'prison worn shirt', decorated with a drawing of a blue butterfly perched on a skeleton's hand.

"We can look back and say that she was simply psychotic," Dixon said. "And it is really easy to dismiss her killings as someone who was simply crazy violent and not read into it anymore than that. But in looking at the ages and gender of the victim, we can see the connection.

All of her victims were old enough to be her mother. So perhaps in Dana's mind she saw her victims as substitutes for her late mother with whom had a lot of anger toward. And I mean violent, aggressive anger. So when she subdued her victims with the phone cord, she would unleash a torrent of rage, smashing them with irons, stabbing them with utility knives,bashing them over the head with wine bottles. She would attack them and have flashbacks of her battles with her Mom, doing things to the victim that she was powerless to do to her mother as a little girl."

"She was doing it all for Mommy."

LEE ANN REIDEL

NIKKI HEFKO

49

What could lead a normal middle class woman to be accused of killing an innocent man? This is the story of convicted murderer Lee Ann Reidel.

Early Years

Lee Ann Reidel, then Lee Ann Armanini, was born in the summer of 1967. Her childhood was very normal. She was the second of four children, to parents David and Pat Armanini. The family lived in a middle class, suburban area in Long Island, New York. Things went well for a few years; they went on regular vacations and spent the holidays together, life was good.

It was when Lee Ann turned 11 that things started to go wrong. Her parents divorced. Pat Armanini, Lee Ann's mother, moved to Florida to live with a new female lover. Lee Ann was left behind in New York. From that point she was raised by her father, David Armanini, who later remarried. Unsurprisingly, these difficult circumstances seemed to have a negative effect on Lee Ann's life and she entered a downward spiral.

Her teenage years were troubled, culminating in a failed marriage at the young age of 19. As a result of this marriage Lee Ann had her first child, a son named Christopher. Lee Ann raised Christopher alone and had the typical struggles of a young, single mother. The main worry was money; some claim that financial insecurities during this period of Lee Ann's life affected her later actions. However, despite some tough times, David Armanini, Lee Ann's father, claims that she was a responsible mother, who put the needs of her son first.

Family Life

The following years passed without incident. Lee Ann didn't have another serious boyfriend until she met Paul Reidel in 1998. The pair met at a Long Island gym where Lee Ann had started working out. They quickly fell in love. Friends of Lee Ann claim that she was very happy. She liked Paul Reidel because he was a strong, muscly man who could protect her, but he also had a gentle nature. The relationship progressed quickly, and soon they were engaged. Cathy Armanini, Lee Ann's stepmother, stated that the family were very pleased when they discovered that the pair had plans to marry.

Paul Reidel had a difficult past – he spent several years in prison on drug dealing charges when he was 19. However, he had since reformed and become a very ambitious man. He opened a business named Dolphin Fitness Club, with his best friend, Alex Algeri. Dolphin Fitness Club in Amityville, New York, was a popular 24 hour gym for weightlifters. The business was thriving and Paul was doing very well financially. Lee Ann appreciated her new lifestyle – she had gone from being a struggling single mother, to the partner of a rich business owner.

Lee Ann and Paul had a church wedding in July 1998. The wedding was quite a lavish display, with impressive decorations and catering. Guests described it as a beautiful fairy tale wedding. No one would ever have predicted the terrible events that were soon to follow.

Marriage Troubles

Not long after they were married, Lee Ann discovered that she was pregnant with her second child. Again, family members were delighted. From the outside everything seemed perfect. However, the stress of owning a 24 hour business and the prospect of being a father was starting to get to Paul. He had started using drugs again and quickly became addicted to crack cocaine.

Pat Armanini, Lee Ann's mother, claims that Lee Ann confided in her about Reidel's drug use and that she was very distressed by it. A number of incidents took place involving Lee Ann driving around during the night, trying to locate Paul and bring him back home. Pat Armanini stated that on one occasion Lee Ann even followed him to the location of a drug deal in order to prevent it from happening. This all happened while Lee Ann was heavily pregnant. Lee Ann wanted to preserve their relationship and help Paul get off drugs. Her mother believes that she thought the new baby would fix things between them, and be the wake-up call that Paul needed to stop taking crack cocaine.

For a short time, this did seem to be the case. Paul became very excited about the idea of having a child, especially when he found out it was a boy. When the child was born, they called him Nicholas. Paul asked his best friend and business partner, Alex Algeri, to be Nicholas' godfather. Algeri happily agreed.

However, despite a happy period, Paul Reidel's drugs habits remained. He continued to use crack cocaine regularly. Lee Ann would apparently find needles and vials around the house, and feared that their small child would end up getting injured or worse. In July 2000, things came to ahead and Paul returned home from work one night to find that Lee Ann, his new born baby and stepson, were gone. Also missing was a large amount of money and possessions from the house. Lee Ann had fled to her mother's place in Florida with the children, taking $120000 with her.

Losing his family seemed to be the wake-up call that Paul Reidel needed. He was afraid that he would no longer be able to see his son. Reidel hired a lawyer to help fight for shared custody of Nicholas and he wanted Lee Ann and the baby to come back to New York while they waited for a custody decision. Paul stated that he wanted to be part of Nicholas' life, and he couldn't do that from so far away. Ultimately though, Reidel did not want his family to fall apart and he spent the next four months trying to reconcile with his wife. He made many promises to Lee Ann during this time. Most importantly, Reidel agreed to go to rehab and ditch his cocaine habit.

Lee Ann and the children eventually returned to Long Island in December 2000. It seemed like the two were trying to sort out their marriage and wanted to try again. Everyone believed that they had gotten over the difficult drugs issues and were now on the path towards happy family life once more. Paul was pleased, he was able to stay in the area of his business, and see his wife and son every day. However, not all was as it seemed and Lee Ann's motivations for returning to Long Island would later be called into question.

The Murder

One month later on the 17th January 2001, an unbelievable act of violence took place. Alex Algeri was shot in the face and killed outside the Dolphin Fitness Club. Gym members and the local community of Amityville were shocked; it was obviously a cold blooded murder.

Like any typical January in New York, the weather was very cold and there was a covering of snow on the ground. It was 7.20 in the evening and already dark. It was Paul Reidel's night off; Alex Algeri was covering the late shift at the gym. During what had so far been a perfectly normal evening, Alex popped out to get a CD from his car for one of the regular aerobics classes. He exited the building through the backdoor. The car park was not well lit and would have been very dark. He went round to the passenger side of the car to collect the CD from the glove compartment. Suddenly, a man jumped out of another vehicle parked nearby. As Algeri turned around, the man shot him several times in the face and neck.

Alex Algeri made it back into the gym trying to get help, but quickly collapsed and was dead before he arrived at hospital.

There was chaos. No one could understand why anyone would want Alex Algeri dead. The consensus was that Algeri was a friendly, popular individual who didn't have any known enemies. For a long time, the police had no leads in their investigation into the murder and people began to wonder if Algeri was really the intended victim.

Rumours spread that perhaps the killer had meant to shoot Paul Reidel instead. After all, Paul was the one with the criminal background. He had taken and dealt drugs for many years, and could have gotten involved with the wrong person. Maybe he had drug related debts, or someone was jealous of his flashy lifestyle. However, at this point there was no evidence that this was the case.

Lee Ann seemed to become panicked after Algeri's funeral. She apparently started asking Paul if it was supposed to be him, and what if she and the baby had been there – what if someone came to their house. Lee Ann convinced Paul that they might be in danger in New York, and that the family should move back to Florida.

Running Away

In 2001, the family did just this. Reidel, Lee Ann and the two children, Christopher and Nicholas, moved back to Florida permanently. Reidel was now the sole owner of the Dolphin Fitness Club and he wanted to remain in charge of the Long Island business. He decided to try and run things from Florida, flying out on regular business trips to check how everything was going. Lee Ann and Paul had plans to build a house for them and their two children in Florida. According to Lee Ann's friend, Mary Hanrahan, Lee Ann and Reidel were both very positive about the move. Reidel apparently spoke excitedly about their plans to build a property and yet again, everything appeared to be going fine for them.

The police in Long Island still had a murder investigation with no leads. Months passed without any new information on the case.

On one of Paul's many business trips to New York he received some unpleasant news from a relative. His relative claimed that every time Paul went out of town, a man went to see Lee Ann at the husband and wife's apartment in Florida. The suspicion was that Lee Ann was involved in an affair.

Reidel quickly dismissed the stories about Lee Ann being unfaithful. He believed that their relationship was stronger than ever because Lee Ann was pregnant again. He even told his relatives that the couple planned to call their new baby Paul, after him. Perhaps some family members had their doubts, but for several months everything went smoothly and Lee Ann and Reidel seemed content together.

A Lead

However, all that was about to change. In November 2001 police arrested a drug dealer in New York, named Michael Hubbard. Hubbard tipped off police that Ralph Salierno and Scott Paget from Florida were involved in the murder of Alex Algeri. Hubbard was trying to help the police and give them the impression that he was cooperating in the hope that his own drug dealing convictions would be dropped.

Police quickly brought in Salierno and Paget for questioning. From the very beginning Paget claimed that Salierno was the one who actually committed the murder and fired the gun at Algeri. Paget stated that he was just the driver. Salierno feigned ignorance about the murder for a while, but when he discovered that Paget had pointed the finger at him, he decided to offer his own rundown of events. In Salierno's story, Lee Ann was the one who came up with the plan to commit a murder, and Salierno was merely trying to follow her instructions.

Salierno confirmed that he and Lee Ann had been having an affair since the first time she moved to Florida in July 2000. Lee Ann's own mother, Pat Armanini, had introduced them, with the idea that Salierno could protect Lee Ann if Paul Reidel ever came to Florida and tried to take baby Nicholas. However, the relationship had developed into something much more. The two had fallen in love and kept seeing each other even when Lee Ann and Reidel were supposedly back together. Salierno claimed that Lee Ann had given him instructions to go to New York and kill Paul Reidel, offering him a potential payment of $100000. Salierno said that the killing of Alex Algeri was a case of mistaken identity.

Paul Reidel and Alex Algeri did not look dissimilar; they were both very strong, muscular men and had similar features. Obviously, they shared the same work place and even drove the same type of car. The murder had also taken place in the poorly lit gym carpark on a dark January evening. A case of mistaken identity did not seem impossible to police. Salierno's story was further backed up when he revealed that he was the father of Lee Ann's third child. This proved to be true, meaning that Lee Ann and Salierno had continued to see each other even after Alex Algeri's murder. So far, Salierno's version of events appeared to be adding up.

After Salierno admitted to killing Alex Algeri, Lee Ann confessed that she had indeed been having an affair with Salierno. The new baby, named Zachary, was his. However, she strongly denied that she had any part in planning her husband's murder. Lee Ann claimed that Salierno must have committed the murder in a fit of jealousy over the fact that the husband and wife appeared to be reconciling, and that Algeri was simply in the wrong place at the wrong time. Lee Ann also said that she had continued the affair with Salierno after Alex Algeri's death because her husband had changed – he was withdrawn and paranoid. She maintained that she had no idea that Salierno was the one who killed Algeri.

The police were put in a difficult situation – they were faced with numerous conflicting stories and very little physical evidence. They concluded that the only option was to let the case go to court and see what the outcome would be. In March 2003 Lee Ann Reidel was also arrested for the murder of Alex Algeri, it was decided that she and Salierno would be co-defendants.

The Trial

In March 2004, Lee Ann and Salierno were tried in the same room at Suffolk County courthouse, and faced the same prosecutors, but the outcome would be decided by two different juries. This is quite an unusual set up. The pair faced several charges including first degree murder, second degree murder and conspiracy to commit murder.

The prosecutor was Assistant District Attorney Denise Merrifield. Merrifield began by establishing that the intended victim was in fact, Paul Reidel, not Alex Algeri. Salierno confirmed this in his admission. The real question was did Salierno act alone, or was he acting on the instruction of Lee Ann?

Many witnesses were called upon during the trial. There was no physical evidence of Lee Ann's involvement so the prosecution relied heavily on the testimony of these witnesses. One notable testimony was from Lee Ann's mother's former lover, Elizabeth Russo. Russo claimed that she and Lee Ann's mother had initially introduced Lee Ann and Salierno with the intention of providing protection to Lee Ann. Salierno was told that if Paul Reidel came to Florida Salierno should threaten him and break his legs. This account suggested that Lee Ann was open to violent acts towards Paul Reidel. Russo clearly implied that she believed Lee Ann was capable of giving the instruction to Salierno to commit murder. Russo's account was particularly important for the prosecution because, unlike most of the other witnesses they called, she was not a criminal.

Scott Paget had already admitted that he drove Salierno back and forth to Long Island, New York on the night of the murder. Paget said that Salierno paid him $3000 dollars to drive the getaway car. He received a lower sentence of 18 years for cooperation with police. He also testified against Lee Ann – though the defence maintained that he could have simply been doing this in order to help his own case. Paget testified that Lee Ann instructed Salierno to kill Reidel. He said that Lee Ann gave Salierno a photograph of Reidel and told him the address of the Dolphin Fitness Club. Although this was a damning testimony, the defence tried to argue that Paget was not a reliable witness due to his own conviction and involvement in the case.

However, Lee Ann's case was damaged further when Michael Paglianti, a Florida drug dealer, was called to give his testimony. He said that he had been present when Lee Ann and Salierno met and discussed breaking Paul Reidel's legs. He also claimed that he had heard Lee Ann say that she wanted Reidel dead. Paglianti corroborated Paget's story by saying that he saw Lee Ann give a photograph of Reidel to Salierno. Finally, Paglianti testified that after the night of the murder and Algeri's funeral, Lee Ann verbally abused Salierno for killing the wrong guy.

Having heard from numerous witnesses, Lee Ann's case was not looking good. However, the defence pointed out that most of the witnesses were criminals and there was still no physical evidence of Lee Ann's guilt. There were some discrepancies with the car that Salierno and Paget drove to Long Island, with no record of who paid for the car, or where they rented it from. Lee Ann's attorney, Bruce Barket, questioned why Salierno had killed the wrong man. Surely, if he was acting on Lee Ann's instruction, he would have known that it was Reidel's night off and that Algeri was working at the club that night.

There was still the question of why Lee Ann would want her husband dead. The prosecution had a simple answer for this – money. They claimed that Lee Ann wanted Paul Reidel out of the picture so that she could start a new life with Salierno whilst living comfortably on Reidel's savings.

The prosecution, Denise Merrifield, believed that Lee Ann already started developing the plan to murder Reidel the first time she was in Florida in July 2000. Merrifield suggested that Lee Ann knew that if the husband and wife remained separated when Reidel was killed, she would be a number one suspect. Merrifield said that Lee Ann then pretended to reconcile with Reidel and moved back to New York, all whilst plotting his murder with Salierno. Her plan was to act like the grieving widow after his death, in order to seem innocent. As Reidel's wife, his fortune would be left to her and she would let some time pass before quietly moving back to Florida to be with Salierno.

Of course, the defence disputed this story. Defence attorney Bruce Barket maintained that Salierno went to New York in a fit of rage upon seeing that Lee Ann and Reidel were back together. Barket stated that Salierno's actions were irrational and not well planned; this is how he ended up shooting the wrong person. According to the defence, Lee Ann was oblivious to the fact that Salierno had killed Algeri and that her only wrong doing was the ongoing affair with Salierno.

In the end, it seemed like the decision could go either way for Lee Ann.

The Decision

The jury deciding the fate of Salierno returned to the court room in just four hours. He was found guilty of first degree murder and Judge Louis Ohlig sentenced him to life in prison with no parole.

Lee Ann's jury took longer to reach a decision. Her defence attorney believed that this was a good sign for her case. However, after four long days, the jury found her guilty too. Lee Ann was held equally responsible for the death of Alex Algeri. On the 28th April 2004, she was sentenced to twenty five years to life. The prosecution did not ask for life without parole for Lee Ann. They did not give any comment on why this was, which was unusual because the judge even stated that he would have happily given a longer sentence to Lee Ann had the prosecution asked for it.

Prosecutor Merrifield told the judge that "Justice has been served here, your honour. She, because of her own greed and evil heart, wanted her husband dead. This defendant is the most self-absorbed defendant I have ever prosecuted."

Bruce Barket, Lee Ann's defence attorney, was very upset by the outcome of the case. This is clear from his response to the decision: "I respect the Jury system. I respect the Jury process. I strongly disagree with the verdict."

Although Lee Ann's attorney claims to respect the Jury process, there has been some criticism of the way the case was handled in court. Some believe that the fact that Lee Ann and Salierno were tried in the same room was actually damaging to Lee Ann's case. The psychology of seeing the pair together, with the knowledge that they had an ongoing affair and a child together, could have affected the Jury's decision. The idea that Lee Ann was guilty of something was already in the minds of the Jury members, perhaps they found it hard to make an objective decision on Lee Ann's guilt in relation to the murder itself.

There was also the fact that the unintended victim of the murder was someone completely innocent and well liked. This caused wide spread anger, even those who did not know Alex Algeri felt that it was a real tragedy and an injustice. People were calling for the death penalty, though this was not requested by the prosecution. The high levels of emotion and anger surrounding the case could also have impacted on the Jury's decision making. It's hard to say if the reaction would have been the same if Reidel had been the one killed. It is possible that it would have been easier for the defence to portray Reidel as someone involved in a criminal lifestyle and Lee Ann as a fearful wife, desperate to escape his control. As Algeri was the victim, the Judge potentially felt a lot of pressure to dish out harsh sentences in an attempt to restore justice.

Alex Algeri was only 32 when he was murdered. His sister, Christie Stoll, told the judge "our brother is gone and the hole in our hearts will never be filled because of [Lee Ann's] greed and hatred of her husband. Even though Lee Ann Reidel wasn't there on the night of January 17th 2001, she just as well might have been. Lee Ann Reidel is just as guilty as Ralph Salierno." After the trial Algeri's father, Salvatore Algeri, said that "justice has been served completely."

Despite the defence claiming no evidence, and the issue raised about the nature of the trial, the widely held opinion is that justice was done and that Lee Ann was guilty for her part in Alex Algeri's murder.

Zachary, Lee Ann's third child, fathered by Salierno, is living with Lee Ann's sister in Long Island. Lee Ann and Reidel's son Nicholas is living with Reidel and no longer has any contact with his mother. Paul Reidel gave an insightful interview on the extremely popular talk show, Larry King live. He said that Lee Ann wanted him dead because she knew he would never stop fighting for access to their son. When asked if he felt lucky to have avoided murder, Reidel said "I don't feel lucky, because I would have took that walk. I would have never asked him to do it, and whatever happened, that's a burden I'll always carry." Reidel explained that his life is in order and his ongoing focus is raising his son. "I feel like I have a severe obligation to be a good man and do the right thing by my son because I feel like I owe that to Alex". King also asked Reidel what his feelings were towards Lee Ann, Reidel said that he did not hate her, but that he was confused and that he felt that she deserved the prison sentence.

Salierno is currently serving his sentence at Attica Correctional Facility in New York. Lee Ann is at Bedford Hills Correctional Facility also in New York. So far, her attempts to appeal have been unsuccessful.

KILL HIM JILL

Sarah Thompson

62

For some, gambling is a special treat - a past-time for birthdays, anniversaries and celebrations. It can be a bonding experience that brings everyone together through either luck, or misfortune. For others, gambling becomes an addiction, where they are willing to lie, cheat and steal in order to get their fix. For the lucky few, gambling can become a lifestyle. This lifestyle is often fraught with drugs, danger, embezzlement, lies and fraud. Like many of the stories that have come before them, the story of Bill Gustafik and Jill Rockcastle is one that would make any big-screenwriter proud. When you put in all the ingredients of drugs, grand theft, a professional poker player, a murder and an attempt at suicide, you get something that sounds so surreal, no one could have lived through it.

The truth is, Jill Rockcastle did live through it - but her husband, tragically, did not. While one's heart may feel the instinctive pull to go out to Jill, the reality is much worse. The story of Bill and Jill is set in Las Vegas, where gambling, drugs and danger go hand-in-hand. In the early morning hours of April 13th in 2007, police received an anonymous tip about a dead body on the 23rd floor of a condominium building. This was only the beginning of a web that would slowly begin to unravel, and make it clear that the story of Jill Rockcastle is almost indistinguishable from the story of Bill Gustafik - you cannot tell one story without the other. They're inseparable, even after death.

Jill Rockcastle and Bill Gustafik seemed like a couple who couldn't be happier. Jill and Bill met not long after Bill had divorced his previous wife in 2000. He had also graduated from chiropractor's school - a long way off from his eventual calling as a professional poker player. Meanwhile, Jill worked in the mortgage business, refinancing people's homes for them. It made her enough money to be independent and happy. Bill and Jill met in the months following his divorce, and hit it off as friends quite well. They started as friends, and stayed this way for about two years. But their relationship started to grow and build quite quickly. They eventually got married in 2005, but their relationship was one of devotion and obsession long before that. It was built on lies, secrets, fraud, and a desire to become better and more fabulous than the lives that they were currently leading.

Their relationship worked because, by Jill's own words, they discovered that they were able to get whatever they wanted out of people. However, their reasons were far different. Jill was able to manipulate the people around her because of what she described as "a need to survive." On the other hand, Bill did what he did out of, what Jill described as, "a need to conquer." In stark contrast to Jill's desires, Bill wanted to to be the most superior and successful person to walk into a room.

Their driving desires were far different, but they worked together all the same. Two master manipulators joined together to form a power couple that would lead them both to their eventual ends. Despite his good life, Bill wanted more. He longed to be one of the richest, most powerful people in the room when he walked in, and Jill was able to help him get it. Jill's inheritance money and her job as a refinancing for mortgages allowed her to live the lavish lifestyle that her partner craved. Even in the beginning of their relationship, the two worked together to manipulate whatever system was set up against them.

The Bill and Jill began their partnership in crime not long after they got together. Bill was going through a custody evaluation with his ex-wife. Both Bill and his ex-wife had been in a custody battle over their nine year old daughter for some time, perhaps all the time that Bill and Jill had known one another. Bill's child support payments would have been $4,000 given to his wife - but Bill asked Jill to re-worked his income in the books so that it looked as if he was being paid less than he actually was. Jill had software that was used to prepare your own tax returns. She showed him that she could alter the returns, and that brought bill out of the rage that had consumed him over the possibility of giving his ex-wife four grand in child support. Jill's solution was a savior - together, Bill and Jill worked their magic to cut down Bill's earnings.

Or was it magic? Jill's life story with Bill was left behind in a ten-page suicide note. While Jill Rockcastle never managed to go through with the planned attempt, the note leaves behind sordid and intimate details of their lives. The beginning of their schemes apparently started with a threat. In her note, Jill describes the first arrangement together, shedding more light on the custody scheme. At first, Jill refused Bill's request to arrange his income so that it looked as if he were earning less than he actually was. But then, Bill began to threaten her. A few days before the court hearing, Jill held the phone against her ear, listening to Bill bellow at her from the other end - screaming about how badly he needed her to do this for him. Like many women in her position, the threats and shouting worked, and Jill conceded to the plan.

And that plan also worked. The morning of the court hearing, Jill gave in and fixed the tax return documents to reflect a much lower income that Bill was truly earning. Their first scheme allowed for Bill to pay only $1,800 in child support - less than half of the proposed amount. In her 10 page letter, Jill wrote, "We began living without rules and not afraid of consequence." After all, what an exhilarating moment - to break the law and get away with it. It's no wonder that Jill and Bill became addicted to the thrill of it all. Not to mention, the money that came rolling in with it.

Bill Gustafik eventually opened up his own office in Antioch. Jill worked there with him, though her job behind the scenes was a bit different. She fixed the books in order to subtly increase the profit made between them. Jill was also instructed by Bill to finance real estate deals for some of the patients that came into Bill's chiropractor's office, in order for the income to go directly to Jill. The money that they made together was more than enough - and at the same time, it was nowhere near enough.

While Bill had his own talents when it came to these schemes, it was Jill who was the mastermind. In 2004, Bill took over one of this offices in Hayward, becoming the owner. Jill was the one who helped him purchase the entire building, and Jill was the one who helped him buy the building as an LLC, so that the purchase would have no effect on his personal credit. Meanwhile, Bill used his own talents in scamming his patients. Person after person, Bill would overcharge and over treat his patients in order to get as much money as possible. While Bill was doing this, it was Jill who was working behind the scenes for him - fixing his books, making sure that Bill was getting even more money than he worked for.

Jill had her own schemes, too. Independent of Bill, Jill Rockcastle worked deals, financing larger homes with large mortgages. On each home, Jill would get 2% or more on each one - that meant on a deal that was $700,000, Jill would take home $14,000. This allowed Jill to work less than Bill. In fact, she only worked once or twice a month. Even $8,000 was more than Jill usually spent in a month. While she was content with their level of riches, Bill wasn't. He wanted more, and with Jill at his side, he was determined to get it.

Bill wanted more of of life - even more than his 7 am to 7 pm lifestyle of scamming patients and fixed books was giving him. Bill began to obsess over getting on television. He wanted to play poker, and he wanted to do so on TV. Despite his already lavish lifestyle, Bill wanted more than just that. He wanted global recognition. Jill went along with it - after all, she had the time, and she has the devotion to Bill.

The note that had been left behind, written in Jill's own words, describes how it was around this time that the two of them went off to Las Vegas together - a city full of glittery lights, casinos, gambling, and eventual devastation. It was in October of 2004 that Jill followed Bill to Las Vegas. As she puts it, their move to Las Vegas was "the beginning of the con." Bill began to live the lifestyle that he believed he deserved - one that was lavish, with extravagant spending. It was Jill who continued to make it all possible, and Jill who continued to watch on. She helped him buy two houses, and get his extravagant car. Everything that Bill had and wanted was because of Jill. Without Jill Rockcastle, he would still be stuck, paying the $4,000 of child support to his ex wife. Bill's desire to be rich in a visible way left Jill vying to make herself worthy of him - she got plastic surgery, enhancing herself to look just like another one of Bill Gustafik glittering trophies.

Jill Rockcastle's letter reveals an even darker side of Bill - one that she, alone, was privy to. There was a time, undisclosed by the note, simply "two years ago", when Jill and Bill had Bill's daughter with them during Christmas time. Jill exposes the man Bill had been. All the time that they had been together, Jill had helped fix everything so that Bill would not have to pay the proposed amount to his ex-wife for child support. Despite Jill's abilities, Bill still wanted to problem gone once and for all. Jill described, in a note to Bill's ex wife, in a chilling lack of detail, that Bill had attempted to have his ex-wife and his ex mother in law killed.

An attempted assassination that didn't go through - the man had taken the money and bolted, leaving Bill both without his money, and Jill with the lasting impression of the lengths that Bill would go to. In Jill's note, she described she believed the Bill felt no love. In her note, Jill says, "He knew deep down that he could not care for someone. [...] he didn't feel love. [...] he didn't feel compassion." This was the man that Jill had been living with for so long. If this man would attempt to put a hit out on his ex wife, there's no telling what he would do to Jill if she didn't continue to fund the lifestyle to which Bill was becoming accustomed.

Jill Rockcastle and Bill Gustafik were living a life that Jill's note described as "the life of fake millionaires". In Las Vegas, Bill finally began to play poker just as he had been obsessing over. The problem arose that Bill wasn't very good. In fact, his first night playing saw that Bill lost nearly ten thousand dollars. Their life together in Las Vegas wasn't everything that it seemed. The money was running out. Together, they were going broke. Their schemes continued on, the con growing and growing, until neither of them had complete control over what they were doing. The new schemes began with getting people to give Jill money. After all, Bill was still struggling with his ex-wife's custody battle. If he obtained more money, it would be scrutinized for child support. So it was Jill who ran the scams, and Jill who brought in the money.

The newest scam to get money was selling fake real estate. Jill allowed the cognitive dissonance get the better of her. Even some of the people who were supposedly their friends fell victim to Bill and Jill - there was nothing and no one that they couldn't con when they put their heads together. All the while, Jill told herself that she was helping out. Even if what they were doing was wrong, Jill was devoted to Bill. She loved him, and she wanted to help him. How could she say no? After all, they had left their lives behind, left behind Bill's doctor's offices, all for the bright light and excitements of Las Vegas. Bill wanted to be a high roller, and for a short while, Jill was rich. She allowed herself to block out the things that they were doing. In her letter, she says, "That's how I lived with my sick self."

But Bill was spending money faster than Jill could bring it it. He began to do drugs, and Jill would watch, dispassionate, as Bill would do lines of cocaine and play online poker. They were running out of money faster than Jill could replenish it. He would play a poker tournament and lose upwards of $15,000. Jill was a gambler as well, but she was better at it than Bill. She wasn't a poker player - rather her game of choice was Roulette. Jill could easily win thousands upon thousands of dollars. But, as quickly as Jill won $20,000 at Roulette, Bill would take it again. She would barely have time to text him of her winnings before he would come from the poker room, take it, and lose it again.

Jill began to squirrel money away. She knew that there was no possible way that they could keep going on like this. She kept money hidden from Bill, giving it to her children - both grown, at the time - if they ever needed it. Bill was beginning to get frustrated and desperate. Jill tucked away her money, and pulled several more scams that kept Bill in earnings to spend and lose. It was Jill who went to the bank to deposit money in order to keep their bills paid while Bill continued hemorrhage winnings. It was always Jill who had to deposit the money. Every once in awhile, Bill would give her cash and have her deposit it in the bank. The money had to look as if it were coming from Jill, least Bill's ex-wife become aware that Bill was skimming on his custody payments.

Jill was starting to breakdown. Her life had been reduced to running scams, telling lies, and bowing to Bill's whims. Jill knew that she had to stop Bill somehow. In her ten page suicide note, Jill describes, "I"m going to skip so many things in an effort to shorten this but my life was a constant hell for the last year. I'm going to skip all the lawsuits [...] All the tax notices. All the bounced checks. All the drugs." It was this hell that drove Jill to feeling as if she was the only one who was able to put a stop to Bill. She made phone calls to friends and other connections, feeling an ever overwhelming desperation. Jill even made a call to her attorney, desperate for someone to help her and get her out of the situation - her attorney only told her that Bill was addicted to gambling, and that the only thing to do is to wait until he has nothing left. But waiting was not something that Jill could, or would, do.

Jill took it into her own hands to stop bill, after having gone to the doctor and found out that the stress of the situation has started to give her shingles. At 7:30 in the evening, police received a call from an anonymous person, telling them of a dead body. When police investigators arrived, they wound Bill Gustafik dead. His body was in the master bedroom, and a kitchen knife was stashed away in the trash bin. The police had very little contention among them about who the suspect could be. Upon first glancing at the scene of the crime, they immediately suspected Jill Rockcastle.

The crime was quick. For Jill Rockcastle, killing her husband was not a drawn out plan, with weeks in the making. Nor was Bill Gustafik's death one that caused the police to go on a chase for their suspect. The night before what Jill called "the incident", the couple got into an argument - like most of the arguments in these days, it was about money. The day previous, Bill was leaving for the Bellagio Hotel, located in Las Vegas. He wanted Jill to pay his buy-ins for a poker tournament, and he wanted her to bring $30,000 for him to use. But Jill didn't bring the money. Either she couldn't get it, or she refused to. When she got to their shared Las Vegas condo, the couple began to argue. But the fight didn't end there. After going to sleep angry, Bill and Jill awoke in the morning to continue the same argument. Bill continued to demand Jill to give him money that he could play with. This time, Bill demanded $7,500 from her. Still, she refused.

Bill's aggression began to build. Jill's fears were starting to become realized. He was threatening to kill her, along with her ex wife. It was then that Jill made an attempt to leave. As she went to leave, Bill physically blocked her with his body. He forced her back from the door and into the kitchen. Jill grabbed a knife from the kitchen to defend herself, fearing for her life. The note described how Jill was afraid that Bill would kill her, just as he had said that he would do. She couldn't escape him, though. He simply kept coming for her, and Jill did what she knew would stop Bill once and for all. She swing the knife into his chest, holding the weapon with both hands. When he went down, Jill still had the knife in her hands. In her own words, Jill says she "just snapped".

Jill stabbed him over fifteen times. Just like that, Bill was gone. There was no grand plan. After years of scamming, scheming, lying and cheating, Jill was done. The story of Bill and Jill ends the way so many women's stories have ended - a dead husband, a knife in their hands, years of fear and abuse behind them. While the story leading up to Bill's death involved so many lies, and so many cons, the story of his death is an anticlimactic one. A death that Bill wouldn't have been proud of - the only thing that made him notable in death was the same that made him notable in life: his wife, Jill. And though Bill had gone out as many men do, stabbed and left for dead, it was Jill Rockcastle that made sure everyone would remember his name, and her own.

After he was dead, Jill cleaned up after herself, cleaned herself up, and fled from the condo. Just like that, Bill Gustafik was dead and Jill Rockcastle was on the run. She had stopped him, just as she knew that she had to do. It was then that Jill Rockcastle disappeared, and on the Monday after Bill Gustafik's death, Jill Rockcastle sent an email to her friends, family and various business partners. The email included ten pages of a suicide note. The note goes in depth on all of Jill's struggles throughout her time of having known Bill, and all of the things that had happened to her. The note describes Bill's struggles with his gambling addiction, and many of the scams and schemes that they had performed today. It was, essentially, ten pages of confessions, implicating herself in all of the things that she and Bill had done together. But, it was always a note to tell everyone goodbye.

In her email, Jill wrote: "This is my final statement done to help all the people affected by my actions [...] and the results of whatever happen to them in our aftermath. I'm writing this so that each person that receives it will identify with the time period in which your experience occurred with him and I and can have some of the why [...] answered. I am not trying in anyway to justify a single thing in here. I am not looking to clear my name or actions. I have already done the most final things possible to stop us from hurting anyone else."

The email was a suicide note, one that was meant to tell everyone that nothing that she and Bill had done would ever touch them again. She alludes here to Bill's death, and to what she had planned to do in order to "stop us" from continuing on how she had been.

Of course, police investigators couldn't let Jill Rockcastle get away with what she had done by allowing her to kill herself. An attempt to find Jill where she had fled was made, first by searching her home in San Ramon that she had kept with Bill. The Las Vegas police called the San Ramon police and urged them to go to the home that Jill and Bill had owned together in San Ramon, in order to arrest her or take her to the hospital, depending on how far she had gone through with her plan to end her life.

However, police investigators were shocked to find that Jill Rockcastle was not in her home in San Ramon. When the police broke down her door, there was no one. Another anonymous call was given to the Las Vegas police, this time urging them on to another location, this time in San Luis Obispo. The call advised them that Jill could be found at a bed and breakfast by the name of Petit Soleil Bed and Breakfast. The San Luis Obispo police searched the small establishment, and found her in her room. She was unconscious, having attempted to end her life with an overdose , just as she had stated that she would in her email.

It was three days after the initial murder when Jill Rockcastle was finally found and apprehended. After the email had gone out, people had begun coming forward with stories of their experiences with Jill Rockcastle and Bill Gustafik. Some people were adamant that Bill didn't deserve what he had got, even if he was a scammer and a cheat. Many people also described Jill has being aggressive herself, with a cocaine habit that matched her husband's. More and more people came forward to tell their stories about how the couple had cheated them out of property and money.

It was Jill's email that had described Bill as aggressive and dangerous, detailing all of the ways in which she was afraid of him. As more people came out of the woodwork as victim's of Jill and Bill, a new light was beginning to be shed on Jill herself. Jim Rivera, one of Bill Gustafik's closest friends from when they were younger, described the Bill in Jill's letter as "inconsistent" with the man that he had known his whole life. Another anonymous friend, this one of Rockcastle, described Jill has being the one to lure Bill into a relationship. Jill was the mastermind, people who knew the couple said. In court, attorneys said that Jill Rockcastle showed no signs of battered woman's syndrome, as both her own public defender and ten page email tried to claim.

Perhaps no one will ever know the truth of what happened between Bill Gustafik and Jill Rockcastle. All that is known is the memories of the couple, the memories of Bill, and the email that had been sent to friends, family and business contacts. Jill had intended to be dead after sending that email, so there is no telling what is truth, exaggeration, or fiction, when Jill did not expect to have to answer for her crime, or the story that she left behind.

JODI ARIAS

JOCELYN BILSON

Society can rest easy knowing that a murderer is safely behind bars for life. It is difficult to pinpoint the exact reason why seemingly innocent people become murderers, but one thing is for certain: a messy relationship can lead to a messy death.

Jodi Ann Arias was convicted by a jury for murdering her ex-boyfriend Travis Alexander. The murder was committed at his home in Arizona in 2008. After breaking up with Arias, he told his friends not to be surprised if "one of these Sundays, I don't show up and you find me dead someplace."

Arias was born on July 9, 1980, in Salinas California. She and her four siblings were raised by their parents, William Angelo and Sandy D. Arias. When she was 10-years-old, she exhibited an interest in photography – a hobby which she enjoyed doing well into her adult years. Her upbringing was not out of the ordinary, but she has spoken of being abused during her childhood years. Arias told reporters that when she was as young as 7-years-old, her parents would hit her with wooden spoons and lash her with a belt. She is a high school dropout who left her formal education when she was in her junior year. She pursued her interest in photography and attempted to go pro while working part-time and moonlighting at various jobs.

In late 2001, Arias began working as a server in a restaurant at the Ventana Inn and Spa in Carmel, California. In 2003, she was romantically involved with the restaurant's food and beverage manager, Darryl Brewer. At the time, the 21-year-old Arias was living in staff housing along with Brewer, aged 41. Brewer told reporters that at the time, Arias was "a responsible, caring, and loving person."

After two years together, the couple bought a house together in Palm Desert, California. They both agreed that the mortgage would be split evenly between the two, totaling at $2,008 per person.

In early 2006, Jodi started her new job working for Prepaid Legal while also working as a part-time server at Ventana. During this time, she also began learning about the Mormon Church and its beliefs, and she invited people from her church to Brewer's and her home for Bible studies and prayer meetings.

It became apparent to Brewer that Arias was taking her faith seriously, and in May 2006, Arias told her live-in boyfriend that she did not wish to continue their physical intimacy since it went against her religious beliefs, and she wanted to get herself ready for her future husband. Strangely enough, this conversation between the couple occurred around the time she got breast implants.

Brewer told reporters that over the summer in 2006, Arias' behavior changed the more she got involved with Prepaid Legal. The once financially responsible person began defaulting on her financial duties and would even miss paying her share of living expenses.

As the months passed, Arias and Brewer's relationship fell apart. He planned to move to Monterrey, California, where he could spend more time with his son from a previous marriage. Arias made different arrangements and instead chose to stay in the house until it was sold. Their relationship officially ended in December 2006, but they would remain close friends who occasionally called each other just to chat. Meanwhile, the house went into foreclosure the following year.

Several months before breaking up with Brewer, Arias met Travis Alexander in Las Vegas, Nevada. He was a motivational speaker and sales rep for Prepaid Legal, and they both ran into each other during a corporate conference in Sin City. At the time, the then-28-year-old Arias was residing in Yreka, California. She was working in sales for the MLM company while trying to build her photography business.

From the beginning, Arias and Alexander were attracted to one another, and after only a week of knowing each other, they began their having sexual relations. At the time, Arias was living in California, and Alexander was in Arizona. During their first months together, they would often travel to other states for both business and pleasure. When they were apart, they took their relationship to the internet and exchanged a total of 82,000 emails. There are also phone transcripts showing that they communicated via phone conversations almost daily.

The entire affair between Arias and Alexander occurred between the months of September and December 2006, while she was still in a relationship with Brewer. In November, Arias was baptized and accepted into the Church of Jesus Chris of Latter-Day Saints. Her decision to join the church was "to get closer to Travis who was a devout Mormon." Two months after her breakup with Brewer, Arias and Alexander began seeing each other exclusively. She moved from her home in California to Mesa, Arizona, to be closer to her new boyfriend.

However, as soon as they became exclusive, they started to experience major relationship troubles. After four months of ups and downs, the couple called it quits in June 2007. Arias provided several different reasons for why they broke up. She initially told people that she simply did not trust Alexander after more time with him as a couple. She later claimed that Alexander was sexually demanding and was both physically and sexually abusive towards her. She even spoke of his wanting her to become his own personal sex slave.

After their breakup, they would occasionally rendezvous to have intercourse. Even while he was dating another woman, he would make time to meet his ex-girlfriend. However, he often complained to close friends that Arias was jealous of the new woman in his life. He alleged that she had slashed his tires on two separate occasions and sent threats using an anonymous email account to both him and the woman he was seeing. He even suspected that while he was asleep, Arias had entered into his home by going through a dog door.

Despite the claims against Arias for stalking and threatening him, they continued to travel together well into March of 2008, and they maintained a physical relationship. At this point in time, Arias became tired of having to sneak around in order to meet Alexander. To make matters worse for their relationship, Arias had to leave the apartment she was sharing with her roommate since her roommate's husband was moving in. After finding no other place to live in Arizona, Arias returned to Yreka, California, where she stayed with her grandparents.

Police documents show that Arias really left Arizona and that Arias and Alexander continued to exchange messages and photos over the internet. Alexander's friends told reporters that in June 2008, he grew tired of dealing with Arias' somewhat insane behavior and jealousy. Alexander suspected that the woman he was cheating with would log into his Facebook account and frequently access his bank statements. This was when he decided to cut ties with Arias for good, and he told her that he wanted her out of his life forever.

On May 28, 2008, Arias and her grandparents reported a burglary that had occurred in their house. A .25-caliber pistol and several other random objects were taken. In the end, the gun was never found.

Arias was planning on driving to Arizona to meet with Alexander. Several days traveling to Arizona, she made several attempts to contact her old boyfriend, Brewer. When she got a hold of him, she asked him to lend her two gas cans for a trip she was going to take. She never returned the cans to Brewer, and receipts showed that she bought another gas can, sunscreen, and skin cream from Walmart in Salinas, California. The purchases were made on June 3, 2008.

Later that evening, she drove to an ARCO gas station in Pasadena, California, where she bought 8.3 gallons of gasoline. The purchase was charged to her debit card, and she purchased another 9.6 gallons using cash. Again, she used her debit card on June 6th: three times in Salt Lake City to buy gas, once at a truck stop in Winnemucca, Nevada, and finally at a 7-Eleven convenient store in Sparks, Nevada.

According to police evidence, Arias went to Redding, California, and rented a Ford Focus on June 2, 2008, from Budget Rent-a-Car. Although he did not want to be involved with Arias any longer, she made the trip from California to Mesa, Arizona, to meet him. They rekindled the flames of their sexual relationship and took pictures of themselves in the middle of intercourse and posing nude.

On June 4th, Arias made the drive back to California, and she returned the rental car on June 7th. Initially, she informed the car rental agency's staff that she was planning on driving the car locally, but she had traveled over 2,800 miles when she returned it. The staff also noticed that all of the floor mats were missing and that there were red stains on the front and back seats. Unfortunately, Budget Rent-a-Car's staff washed and cleaned the car's interior before police could inspect it.

Phone records show that after June 4th, Arias made numerous phone calls to Alexander's phone and left voicemail messages. Her excuse for contacting and leaving voicemails on his phone was because he did not meet his promise to come visit her in May.

Several days after their last meeting, Alexander's friends became worried about him when he did not attend an important business meeting, and when he did not show up for their trip to Cancun, Mexico. Two of Alexander's work friends from Prepaid Legal Services went to his apartment on June 9th to check up on him. They met one of Alexander's roommates who insisted that Alexander was not in, and he had been out of town for several days.

The co-workers and roommate searched the apartment and found a key to Alexander's bedroom which was locked. Inside, they found him on the ground of his bloody shower stall. An autopsy was performed and determined that he had a gunshot wound in his brow, was stabbed between 27 and 29 times, and his neck had been slit. It was determined that the murder of Alexander had occurred on June 4, 2008 – a full five days before discovering his corpse.

Investigators went to the apartment and collected several important pieces of evidence at Alexander's murder scene. While inspecting the bathroom, an empty .25 caliber round was found near the sink. Another crucial piece of evidence was a seemingly brand new digital camera that was found in the tub of his apartment room's washing machine. To inspectors, it appeared as if the camera had gone through a washing cycle, possibly in an attempt to break the camera and memory card.

Many people who knew Alexander were aware of his growing annoyance at Arias' stalking tendencies. The person who called the police and alerted them to Alexander's death even suggested to investigators that Arias might be involved in the case. During interviews with the police, Alexander's close friends and family members repeatedly told them to interview Arias.

Esteban Flores, the lead detective in charge of handling the case, received phone calls from Arias, both inquiring the details of Alexander's death as well as offering assistance to help with the investigation. Arias claimed that she had not known about the shooting and stabbing death of her ex-boyfriend and the last time she had seen him was back in April 2008.

Eight days after police found Alexander's body on the floor of his apartment, Arias was swapped for DNA and fingerprinted. Many of Alexander's friends also volunteered to be swabbed and fingerprinted.

Two days later, Arias was questioned by investigators concerning a collection of photos that had been recovered from the memory card of digital camera discovered in the washing machine. The photos were time-stamped on June 4, 2008, and showed images of them having sex, of Alexander standing in the shower stall, possibly only minutes before he was shot and stabbed. In addition, there were several photos of Alexander lying down on a pool of blood.

Investigators recovered deleted photos of Arias posing nude and in provocative positions for the camera. Those photos were also time-stamped on June 4, 2008. A week later, laboratory tests concluded that a bloody print discovered at the scene of the crime contained DNA that fit Arias' and Alexander's. It was also concluded that Arias'

DNA matched with a strand of hair found nearby Alexander's corpse. Despite the growing evidence linking Arias to being there on the suspected date of Alexander's death, she continued to claim that their last meeting was in April.

A memorial service was held for Alexander several weeks after his death, and Arias attended the service to pay her respects. She wrote a long sympathy letter addressed to Alexander's grandmother, had flowers delivered to his family, and wrote on her MySpace page about how she loved and missed him.

One month after the body of Alexander was found – coincidentally, on her 28th birthday – a grand jury in California accused and charged her with first-degree murder. On July 15th, she was arrested and kept in jail until September when she was finally extradited to Arizona for her trial.

While incarcerated and awaiting trial in Arizona, she gave reporters two different versions of her whereabouts at the time of Alexander's death. First, she told The Arizona Republic newspaper that she was not involved in the killing of her ex-boyfriend. She claimed innocence but no explanation as for why traces of her DNA were found at the scene of his death.

On September 24, 2008, she admitted to TV reporters from Inside Edition that she was with Alexander when he was brutally murdered, but she alleged that two intruders had broken in and shot then stabbed him.

She retold the second version of events to the true-crime series 48 Hours that her life was saved by a jammed gun. During the "home invasion," Arias last saw Alexander in his room with a new digital camera. Moments later, a loud gunshot rang, and Arias flung herself to the bathroom floor. After looking up, she saw a masked man and woman in all-black apparel approaching her. Arias claimed that the man had pointed the gun he used to shoot Alexander at her, but the gun jammed after he pulled the trigger. She reported that she immediately ran out of the house, leaving Alexander behind and did not look back.

In her second version of her whereabouts, she alleged that she did not alert the police out of fear for her life. In her fear, she decided to pretend that nothing out of the ordinary had happened and immediately jumped in her rented Ford Focus and drove back to her grandparent's house in California.

After a lengthy pre-trial and jury selection processes, her trial began on January 2, 2013. Due to the previous statements that Arias provided to the public and the media, her case was well-known throughout Arizona and California, and it was even aired live.

In the opening arguments, Juan Martinez – the prosecutor – was asking for the death penalty for Arias for murdering her ex-boyfriend. Arias' appointed defense counsel countered that it was a justifiable homicide since it was done in self-defense. Several graphic photos were flashed across the courtroom televisions for the jury and attendees to see. There were pictures of Arias' nude body taken by Alexander that were time-stamped just minutes before pictures showed his mangled body on the floor of his shower stall, his mouth and nose filled with blood, and with a large gash in his throat.

A man testified in court that Arias had visited him on June 5th, 2008, in Utah. He noticed that her hands were bandaged, and when he asked her about it she said that she had received cuts after handling broken glass working as a server at a restaurant in Yreka, California. The name of the restaurant was "Margaritaville," but a detective testified that there was no restaurant called "Margaritaville" in Yreka.

Based off the of the evidence provided by police regarding a burglary in Arias' grandparents' home where a .25-caliber pistol was taken one week before they found a spent .25 caliber round in Alexander's bathroom, the prosecution said that the two findings were linked. Prosecutors argued Arias staged a burglary in the home where she was staying with her grandparents, stole the gun, and used it to shoot and murder Alexander in his bathroom.

After 14 days, the prosecution ended its case on June 16, 2013, when Martinez confronted one of the defense's witnesses concerning Arias' "moral character." He surprised the witness when he flashed the nude photos of Arias and the bloodied body of Alexander. After this, the trial was on hiatus for 10 days. In the meantime, attorneys from both sides argued about how the case would progress.

On February 4th, 2013, Arias came to the stand in her own defense. She was cross-examined for 18 long days, and the time she spent on the stand was called "unprecedented" by viewers and attorneys. On the first day of her lengthy testimony, Arias disclosed that she was abused emotionally and physically by her parents at an early age. She then testified that she, in fact, did rent a car from Budget Rent-a-Car in Redding, California, with the intent to drive to Arizona to meet Alexander.

On the second day, she told the court about the nature of her relationship with Alexander. The plan was to depict Alexander as sexually deviant. She spoke of how their sex life included both oral and anal sex; the latter being a painful experience in the beginning, but technically not against the rules of sexual conduct in her their Mormon beliefs. A phone tape was played for the jury, in which Alexander spoke of wanting to zip-tie Arias to a tree while she wore a Little Red Riding Hood costume. She later testified that Alexander had pedophilic tendencies and he was secretly sexually attracted to young boys and girls.

As her testimony went on, she described her relationship with Alexander to be both physically and emotionally abusive. In one instance, she retold an especially traumatic experience where Alexander shook and screamed at her, and then body slammed her to the floor. He then kicked her in the chest before resuming his verbal tirade. While showing a crooked ring finger to the jury, she said she attempted to block the kick with her hand.

Arias then told a third and final version of what happened on the day of Alexander died. Arias said that their dysfunctional relationship reached its boiling point when she shot Alexander in self-defense. She claimed that she pulled the trigger when he became furious after a day of sexual intercourse and after she had dropped his newly purchased camera. She did not intend to kill him, but she felt that she was forced to fight back.

Due to the inconsistencies in her retelling of what happened on the day of Alexander's death, both prosecutors and observers questioned her credibility as a witness. This thought was relayed by William Zervakos, the foreman of the jury panel, who told ABC reporters, "I think she was not a good witness."

On March 14th, Richard Samuels, a psychiatrist who diagnosed Arias with post-traumatic stress disorder, took the stand on behalf of the defense. He said that she was in a "flight or fight" mode at the time of Alexander's death, possibly suffering from a case of acute stress at the time. He took the stand for six days while the prosecutors drilled him with questions and the judge read a list of questions prepared by the jurors. When asked whether this scenario could have occurred without a preplanned notion of committing murder, he responded that it was possible but not probable.

On March 26th, Alyce LaViolette, a psychotherapist who specializes in cases of domestic violence and abuse, testified on behalf of the defense. She told the court Arias exhibited common traits of shame and humiliation often experienced by victims of domestic abuse. Similar to Samuel's time at the witness stand, she was cross-examined by prosecutors and answered a list of 160 questions made by the jurors which mainly focused on Arias' credibility as a witness.

On May 4th, the two sides offered their closing statements. The defense argued that there was no premeditated aspect to the killing of Alexander, and "if [Arias] is guilty of any crime, it is the crime of manslaughter and nothing more." Martinez gave his rebuttal, saying that "there is no evidence that [Alexander] ever laid a hand on [Arias], ever. Nothing indicates that this is anything less than a slaughter. There is no way to appease this woman who just wouldn't leave him alone."

On May 8th, after three jurors were dismissed from their duties for misconduct, health reasons, and for being arrested for a DUI offense, Arias was found guilty and charged with first-degree murder. Seven of the jurors found her guilty of both first-degree premeditated murder and felony murder. The news of her conviction brought tears of joy to Alexander's family, and people outside of the courtroom celebrated by chanting and cheering.

On May 15th, following Arias' conviction, the prosecution, who was seeking the death penalty, had to convince the jury that the murder committed was "cruel, heinous, and depraved." The only witness available to testify was a medical examiner who assisted with the autopsy on Alexander's body. Before the aggravation phase began, Arias' defense attorneys repeatedly asked to be relieved of the case but were available to give brief opening and closing arguments, in which they claimed that the adrenaline rushing throughout his body probably prevented him from feeling pain when he was shot. After about three hours of deliberation, the jury decided that Arias was eligible to receive the death penalty.

May 16, 2013, marked the beginning of the penalty phase for Arias. The prosecution called members of Alexander's family to the stand to deliver their impact statements. Five days later, Arias pleaded for her life and requested a life sentencing opposed to capital punishment. The reasons she cited for preferring the former to the latter is because she did not want to give any more grief to her family. "Whatever they come back with," Arias said to reporters of the Arizona Republic, 12 News, and NBC's Today, "I will have to deal with it. I have no other choice… [The verdict] felt like a huge sense of unreality; I felt betrayed, actually, by the jury. I was hoping they would see things for what they are. I really felt awful for my family and what they were thinking."

On May 23, 2013, the judge declared a mistrial in the sentencing phase. The jury could not come to a unanimous decision between the death penalty and a life sentence, and the vote ended in 8-4 in favor of the former. After it was ruled a mistrial, the jury foreman told reporters why the jury was torn between the two sentences. "We're charged with presuming innocence, [but] she was on the stand for so long [that] there were so many contradicting stories." He further spoke of how the deliberation process was emotionally and physically overwhelming for the jury and how they were horrified when the judge declared a mistrial after all of their efforts. "By the end of it, we were mentally and emotionally exhausted… When we found out that they had actually called a mistrial… we felt like we had failed."

The retrial began in October 2014 with a new jury being presented the same evidence from the first trial. This time, there was greater emphasis on the psychological makeup of both Alexander and Arias. The defense portrayed Arias as a vulnerable woman who responded naturally against the physically abusive Alexander. On April 13, 2015, she was free of the death penalty and was sentenced to life without parole after 25 years.

Jodi Arias is currently in the Arizona State Prison Complex where she will spend the remainder of her life. While behind bars, Arias had gained a considerable fan base and would receive weekly marriage proposals. Ben Ernst, an obsessed fan who had been following Arias' trial closely, began corresponding and talking to her on the phone three times a week. They soon became a couple and in 2016, planned to get married, despite her inmate status with no possibility of parole. They plan on having children together, although conjugal visits in an

Arizona prison are unheard of. Whatever drew him to her in the first place is a mystery, but he can rest easy knowing that he won't meet the same fate that Alexander met 10 years ago.

KILLER NIECE: THE TRUE STORY OF VERNICE BALLENGER

MARY EASTON

In 1983, Vernice Ballenger, with the help of her estranged husband Mac Ballenger and two other men, arranged the robbery and subsequent murder of her elderly aunt Myrtle Ellis. Her motive was simple—money.

It all began earlier that year, when Myrtle Ellis was involved in a car accident. She was taken to the hospital, where a rather unusual discovery was made. Ellis had $60,000 in cash on her person. This large sum of cash made headlines. Local newspapers ran stories on the odd occurrence. These stories caught the eye of Ellis's niece, Vernice Ballenger.

Believing that the elderly Ellis likely still had the cash, Ballenger devised a plan to rob her aunt and get the money. She enlisted the help of her estranged husband Mac Ballenger, who hired two acquaintances to rob Ellis in her home. However, they were unable to get the money and instead resorted to violence, murdering Ellis and setting fire to her home.

The crime went unsolved for years, until the wife of one of the men involved went to the police.

This is the story she told...

Early Life

Vernice Ballenger (born Alston) was born to Verner F. Alston and Marguerete Raspbery Alston in Carthage, Mississippi in 1937. She was the second of two children as she had an older brother, R.V. Alston.

Ballenger's early years appear to have been unremarkable. She remained in Leake County Mississippi and married Mac Ballenger. The couple would three children—one boy and two girls. In 1970, Vernice's brother R.V. Alston died tragically at the age of 35.

"Vernice was on the plump side," journalist Mark Crist said. "She had a perpetual frown on her face and wore rainbow colored moo-moos around the house. She had red hair and had an intense stare that could intimidate. But her bark was worse than her bite as she was on the cowardly side when push came to shove."

Mac and Vernice eventually separated. Mac moved to Greenville, Mississippi while Vernice remained in Leake County. They did not formally divorce however, and remained legally married, with Vernice keeping the last name Ballenger.

"There wasn't much doing in Leake County," Crist said. "The typical weekend for a woman was to go to the hair salon on Saturday and church on Sunday. That was Vernice's life and she didn't seem to want any more than that. Until she read about her aunt Myrtle."

Crime

Aunt Myrtle Involved in Car Accident

In 1983, Vernice Ballenger happened to read in the newspaper that her elderly aunt, Myrtle Ellis, was involved in a car accident. Ellis was injured, but her wounds were not life-threatening. She was taken to the hospital, where nurses discovered something odd—Ellis had $60,000 (roughly $145,000 in 2016 when adjusted for inflation) in cash with her at the time of the accident. The reason why is unclear, but the story was strange enough that it made the local newspapers along with reports of the car wreck.

While some may have argued that broadcasting the fact that this elderly woman, who lived alone in the country, had such a large sum of cash, could threaten Ellis's safety, it was done regardless. This oversight by local reporters proved to be fatal for Myrtle Ellis.

"It seemed hare-brained at the time to broadcast the fact that she had so much money," Crist said. "It really gives you an idea of how hard-up that small town of Carthage, Mississippi was for news. It was a small, rural town with one main street. Nothing happens there. But when an elderly woman is in a car accident has a lot of cash on here, that makes the news. It also invited an opportunist in Vernice Ballenger."

When Vernice Ballenger read about her aunt's accident and the large sum of cash she had on her at the time, her interest was piqued. Ballenger went to visit her aunt, intending to find out what she had done with her money since the car accident.

"Myrtle Ellis was a nice, sweet elderly woman," Crist said. "She lived alone out in the country. She spent her days sewing dolls and drinking tea. Didn't have a care in the world and would have no reason to suspect her own niece of coming over to steal her money."

Feigning concern for her aunt's safety, Ballenger asked about the money. Ellis informed her that she had put the hospital had taken the money and put it into a bank account for Ellis, where it was safely stored at that time.

"Vernice probably gave little thought as to how her aunt Myrtle came up with that kind of money," Crist said. "She just wanted it and would do anything to get it."

Despite Ellis's assurances that the money was now in the bank, Ballenger still believed her aunt had the money in the house or on her person somewhere. Far from being the concerned niece she pretended to be, Ballenger was in fact plotting to rob Ellis and take the money.

"Her aunt was telling the truth," Crist said. "But Vernice was so focused on getting some money that she completely ignored the fact that her aunt was telling the truth. That was the kind of mindset she had, once she believed one thing, in this case the idea that her aunt was still holding the money, she could not change her focus. Vernice lacked the silver-tongued harm of other female killers. She could not have manipulated her aunt into giving her the money. She would have to take it by force."

Planning the Crime

But Ballenger couldn't do it herself—after all, her aunt would recognize her. Instead, Ballenger sought the help of her husband, Mac Ballenger. Despite the fact that the couple was separated, Ballenger believed her estranged husband would be financially desperate enough to help her commit the crime. She drove to Mac's house in nearby Greenville, MS and asked him for assistance with the robbery. Mac refused, possibly believing that Ellis would recognize him as well, but told Ballenger he knew someone who would be willing to do it.

Mac enlisted the help an acquaintance of his, whom he believed would help commit the robbery, James Head. On July 9, 1983, Mac drove to Vernice's home in Leake County, where she lived with the couple's two daughters. Head arrived separately and brought a friend, Ronald Ritter, to help with the robbery.

"James Head was a local scumbag," Crist said. "The kind of guy who knows all the wrong people because he is 'wrong people'. Ritter was a huge guy. Muscular and intimidating with a beard and sleeveless shirts to show off his biceps. It took these two guys to rob an old lady."

The group met a second time at the Vernice's home the following morning, July 10, 1983. Here they would devise a plan for the robbery that ultimately led to the murder of Ballenger's aunt, Myrtle Ellis. Ballenger told Head and Ritter about the car accident and the $60,000 her aunt had had on her person at the time. She even told the men how Ellis had insisted she had since put the money in a bank account.

However, Vernice told her new co-conspirators that she did not believe her elderly aunt. She told Head and Ritter that Ellis likely still had the money somewhere in the house. She insisted that if Ellis did not give up the money, they should search the house. According to later testimony from Ronald Ritter, Balleger "said that she knew that [Ellis] had it, that if she didn't have it sewed in her brassiere, it would probably be inside of a chair, or something. She had a doll. It might be sewed up in the doll." Vernice encouraged the men to tear apart the house if Ellis did not give up the money willingly.

Vernice also agreed to give James Head and Ronald Ritter each $10,000 for their help with the crime, presumably thinking she could keep the other $40,000 of her aunt's money for herself and her husband, Mac. At this time, the three men and Ballenger had all agreed that they were only going to rob Ellis. According to all involved, they did not intend to hurt Ellis, and Vernice specifically told the men not to harm her aunt.

"Vernice knew her aunt's habits inside and out," Crist said. "She told them how the door was always open and exactly where she would be sitting when they entered the home. She gave them tips on how to terrorize the money out of her aunt but gave explicit instructions not to hurt her. Just to do enough to get the money from her."

Robbery Attempts

That same day, July 10, all four participants—Mac, Head, Ritter, and Vernice—drove to Ellis's house to scope it out and plan the crime. Ellis's house was located in a fairly isolated part of the country outside the more populated center of Leake County. The house was surrounded by a wooded area, making it even more isolated. The group returned together back to Ballenger's house to further discuss their plans before Head and Ritter would go back out to the house on their own to rob Ellis.

Head and Ritter drove to Ellis's house, intending to rob her and leave. However, as they drove through the woods and approached Ellis's home, they saw a hunter in the woods. Head and Ritter were frightened, believing they may have been spotted and that the hunter would later be able to identify them as the perpetrators of the planned robbery. The two men turned around and returned to Ballenger's home where Mac and Vernice were waiting.

When they returned and explained the situation to the Ballengers, Mac insisted that Head and Ritter were just scared. In order to loosen them up, Mac opened up a bottle of whiskey and the men began to drink. Head in particular drank rather heavily. The group discussed their plans further, agreeing once again that they would not harm Ellis, and Head and Ritter agreed to return to Ellis's house and go through with the robbery. This time, it was decided that Mac would go with them as well.

Before they left, Vernice Ballenger gave Head and Ritter a pistol and a rifle. Despite reassurances that they were not going to hurt the elderly Myrtle Ellis, the men took the guns with them. Curiously, Mac made no mention of the guns in his later confession to the police and statements in court, despite admitting to all other aspects of the crime.

Mac, Head, and Ritter made another trip to Ellis's house. By this time, the men had been drinking quite a bit. When they arrived at Ellis's house, Head and Ritter entered the house. Head had the pistol with him. Mac stayed outside, waiting on the porch for the other two men to come back out with the money.

Upon entering the house, Head and Ritter found Ellis and demanded that she give them the money. Ellis told the men she did not have any money in the house. She repeated what she had told to her niece, Vernice, telling the men that the money was not in the bank.

Head and Ritter became angry—Head, according to Mac and Ritter, was a large man and a violent drunk. Ritter first slapped Ellis, demanding that she tell him where the money was. Ellis became angry, insisting that she didn't have any money in the house. She told the robbers once again that the hospital had taken the money after her accident and put it into a bank account for her.

However, Head and Ritter either did not believe Ellis's story or were so infuriated by their failed robbery that they turned to violence. Head began hitting Ellis, knocking her unconscious. Even after Ellis lost consciousness, Head continued asking her questions, demanding to know where the money was. The later autopsy report revealed that Head beat Ellis severely, hitting her in the chest with a great degree of force.

Head pulled out the pistol, put it to Ellis's head and pulled the trigger, intending to kill her then and there. The gun was unloaded, however, and so Head began to beat Ellis with the gun, too. According to Ritter, Head went crazy, beating Ellis senselessly.

"We can't mitigate the perp's actions by blaming it on the alcohol," Crist said. "These men were pure scum. Slime balls of the highest order to beat and maul a defenseless old woman."

Convinced that the money was hidden somewhere on Ellis's person or in the house, Head and Ritter tore apart the house. Vernice had told the men the money was most likely sewn into Ellis's bra or a chair in the house. When Ellis's body was found later, her clothes were partially ripped, indicating that the men had perhaps searched her bra for the money as instructed by Ballenger. However, they were still unable to find the money, and eventually they gave up their search.

Meanwhile, outside the house, Mac searched Ellis's truck outside and found a doll, which Ballenger had also told the men might have the money sewn into it. Mac entered the house and told the men he had found the doll and believed it might contain the money. Head threw Ellis across the room and kicked her one last time, then the men left, leaving Ellis behind in the house.

All three men got back into their van, and Mac gave the doll to Head. Head tore the doll open, searching for the money, but found nothing. He threw the doll out the window and the men drove back to Ballenger's house.

Plotting the Murder

When the men returned to the house, Vernice asked them about the robbery. The men explained that they had been unable to find the money and told Ballenger what they had done. Ballenger was concerned. According to Ritter, she told the men that if Ellis had seen the van or seen Mac, she would know that Ballenger had been involved. Ritter stated that Vernice felt, "if [Ellis] seen Mac or anybody; she would know that Vernice was tied into it, so [we] couldn't leave the situation like that. Said we would have to kill the woman."

"Vernice did a total three-sixty," Crist said. "She realized that if her aunt had seen her vehicle outside the window that she would inform the police. So despite getting nothing out of the whole episode she ordered her 'hitmen' to go back and 'take care of' her aunt. Cold-hearted stuff."

She told the men they would have to burn down the house with Ellis in it in order to hide the evidence and avoid being caught. The group devised a new plan—Vernice Ballenger, Head, and Ritter would return to the house. They would drop Head off and he would start the fire. Then Ritter and Ballenger would return and pick up Head, then leave.

Ritter and Ballenger dropped off Head and drove down the road to wait. When they didn't see smoke coming from the house, Ballenger told Ritter that one of them would have to return to the house to make sure Head had started the fire. Ritter volunteered to be the one to return to the house and ensure it was burned down.

Ritter went back to Ellis's house to burn it down himself. According to his testimony later, Ritter planned to get Ellis out of the house before he burned it down, contrary to the group's original plan.

"While all of this was happening, Aunt Myrtle was dragging herself out of the house," Crist said. "So this was a remarkably tough woman with a strong constitution. She was beaten and bloodied. Her nose and mouth were bleeding. Her eyes swelling and she was having difficulty breathing. Despite all of that, she crawled out of her home and made her way outside. Somehow, someway, she had to get help. But she didn't find it fast enough. The men were on their way back."

Ritter found Ellis lying on the ground outside her home. He entered the house and found a pile of clothes on the floor. Ritter lit a match and threw it on the clothes, starting the fire.

"The men thought that Aunt Myrtle was already dead," Crist said. "If they thought she was still alive they would have most likely beat her to death or dragged her inside the house and set it on fire. Instead, they let her be."

Head, Ritter, and Ballenger all returned to Ballenger's house. Head and Ritter went back to Greenville, MS. Ballenger and Mac remained at Ballenger's home.

The fire department soon responded to the fire at Ellis's home. When they arrived, firefighters found the home burning. Ellis, however, had awoken at some point after the beating and dragged her badly beaten body outside. When firefighters and volunteers got to the scene, they found the now unconscious Ellis lying outside the house near a shed.

Although she had escaped the fire, Ellis was in bad shape and it was immediately clear she had been the victim of a brutal attack. Her head was swollen from the beating she had received at the hands of Head and Ritter and her clothes had been ripped. Ellis already had bruises forming on her body, and she was covered in dirt from dragging herself out of the house and through the yard.

"When the first responders arrived on scene," Crist said. "They immediately asked Myrtle if she knew who did this to her. She hesitated. She said that she knew who did it but did not want them to get into any more trouble than they already were. That was the kind of woman she was. She knew that it all led back to her niece, Vernice. She still played the role of a doting aunt even though she was beaten half to death."

Ellis's Death

Myrtle Ellis was transported to the hospital in Madden, MS, a nearby small town. Ellis remained unconscious the entire time she was in the hospital in Madden. Some time later, she was transferred to University Hospital in Jackson, MS to be treated by a neurologist.

While at University Hospital, Ellis briefly regained consciousness. She was questioned by police, who attempted to learn the identity of her attackers. However, Ellis once again refused to reveal the identity of the people who attacked her. Either out of fear or loyalty to her niece, Ellis never told the police what she knew. She survived for several days in the hospital, but ultimately succumbed to her injuries on July 20th, 1983 in University Hospital.

"She died a painful death," Crist said. "Miraculously, she survived for ten days after the beating as her entire chest cavity was smashed in. Unfortunately, she did not spill the beans on who did. It may seem like a forgiving act but the people involved looked at the prospect of getting away with the crime and possibly committing similar crimes in the future."

After Ellis died, an autopsy by William Featherson was performed to determine the cause of her death and search for any possible clues that would help police solve the crime. In the report, Featherson found that while there were some head injuries, including evidence of a possible hemorrhage in the brain, these injuries were not what killed Ellis.

Additionally, Featherson found extensive injuries in Ellis's chest area. These were likely due to the beating that Head gave Ellis, including throwing her across the room and kicking her. Ellis's four upper ribs on both her left and right side were fractured. Her breastbone was fractured as well, and her mammary artery, which runs alongside the breastbone, was torn.

This torn artery led to massive internal bleeding. Blood filled the right side of Ellis's chest, and according to Featherson, "collapsed her right lung and then pushed the heart and the left lung over into the left side of the chest cavity, and that, the hemorrhage and the displacement of the internal organs, is what produced her death." Featherson also said these injuries led him to believe she had been hit or kicked in the chest, and this attack caused her death.

Most damning of all, Featherson found no injuries caused by fire. This left investigators searching for the person, or people, who had brutally attacked this elderly woman in her home. But they found nothing. The only clue was the sighting of a van near Ellis's home around the time of the attack. This was, of course, Vernice's van. Police tracked down the van and Mac Ballenger confirmed that it belonged to his wife, Vernice Ballenger. However, Ballenger had since had the van painted and put new tires on. The trail of evidence went cold and it seemed Ellis's killers would never be brought to justice.

"The interrogation should have been a lot stronger," Crist said. "With some crack police work, they could have found out how Mac was connected to Ritter and Head. The police simply played their hand too early. They were investigators in a small town and really unused to this kind of brutality and conniving."

An Accidental Confession

Though it seemed for nearly a decade that this heinous crime would go unsolved forever, this turned out not to be the case. In fact, nine years later, the case was cracked wide open by one woman's slip of the tongue. In 1992, police went to the house where James Head lived with his wife. They were only there to serve civil papers entirely unrelated to the murder of Myrtle Ellis.

When they arrived at the home, Head's wife was present. She saw the uniformed police officers in her front yard approaching the house and immediately blurted out, "You're here about that murder my husband committed in 1983." This, according to Leake County prosecutor Mark Duncan, is what "got the ball rolling".

From this initial confession, police were able to arrest all four conspirators, including the mastermind behind this vicious crime, Vernice Ballenger. Mac Ballenger, James Head, and Ronald Ritter confessed to the crime, giving police the full story of how they had planned and executed this robbery gone wrong. Both Mac and Ritter also testified against Ballenger during her murder trial.

"Each of the men had pointed the finger at Vernice," Crist said. "There was no loyalty there. They would all get life sentences in the end."

Vernice Ballenger was found guilty of robbery and capital murder for her role in the killing of Ellis. In January of 1993, she was sentenced to death for her crime. Ballenger made several appeals, but her conviction was never overturned. Her accomplices were all sentenced to length prison terms, but only Ballenger was given the death penalty for her actions. Prosecutors stated that this harsh penalty would serve as a message to others in the area that crimes like Ballenger's would not be tolerated.

However, Ballenger was never given the death penalty. Instead, she died in prison of natural causes in 2002 at the age of 65.

"Vernice was fond dead in her prison cell," Crist said. "She lived out her last days alone and died alone. It was the epitome of a senseless act of violence that got her to where she was."

While it was not the punishment ordered by the court, Ballenger's death brought an end to the tragic case of Myrtle Ellis's murder.

bonus story:

In the early 1960s, Myra Hindley took her first job out of school at a small chemical company called Millwards Merchandise. A shy eighteen-year-old, she kept to herself, reading in the office courtyard during breaks.

But she only did this to attract her co-worker, Ian Brady.

Brady would spend his breaks reading books. Myra soon followed suit in the hopes that he would approach.

After several months, the Glasgow, Scotland native finally made his move.

They both worked at the office as clerks. Brady was four years older than her as they began to date.

Myra lived with her grandmother and gave her virginity to the awkward co-worker on her grandmother's sofa. She would soon become Brady's accomplice in some of the most gruesome child killings in the history of Great Britain.

A BAD NEWS CHARACTER

Brady already had a police record for petty theft. He also had a strange demeanor, tilting his head oddly at people as he stared them down with hooded eyes.

He was nicknamed "Lassie", not a reference to the Collie dog but to his feminine body language. Brady was tall, skinny and would indicate later that he was a bisexual. As a child, he had few friends and was called "Dracula" in the neighborhood. He would torture kittens and see how long it took for them to die.

They were both bookworms and Brady would give Myra books on the Marquis De Sade, trying to introduce her to the world of sexual sadism. After their dates, he would invite her back to his place and play back recordings of Adolph Hitler's speeches.

The young couple would come up with pet nicknames for each other. Myra would call Ian "Hetty" after a character in the Goons and he would call her "Hess" after Hitler's deputy. They would soon become inseparable, both strangely odd people that felt that were superior and set apart from everyone else.

It soon became clear, however, that Ian was influencing Myra and not the other way around. He was her guide to the world of sexual sadism and then later, slowly revealed his desire to rape and murder children.

He started this by sharing a book in the same way he introduced her to sadomasochism. The book had detailed the "crime of the century". A child was the victim and one of the characters was named Myra.

"He had given me a book called 'Compulsion'," Myra recalled. "Which was the story of Leopold and Loeb. They decided to commit the perfect murder. They were studying the philosophy of Nietzsche, his theory of the superiority of the pure Aryan and the strong overcoming the weak. It was very much the Nazi philosophy. They kidnapped a twelve-year-old boy for a ransom. They killed him, were caught and sent to prison. I told him it was a very disturbing book. But why exactly had he wanted me to read it? He told me he wanted to do a perfect murder and I was going to help him. That was why he needed me to pick someone up as I was a woman and a child would be more trusting of a woman. I burst into tears and he slapped my head backward and forward. I managed to fight him off and told him to stop it."

Myra fell prey to Ian's system of push and pull psychology. He would be abusive to Myra then inexplicably turn around and be sweet to her.

"I must be totally honest and say he wasn't always cruel and sadistic towards me," Myra said. "We had some pleasant times in country places that he'd found during his travels on his bike. We'd pack a picnic lunch, lots of coffee, bottles of wine and spend whole days in peace and tranquility. That was such a contrast to the other side of him. These were moments I treasured and thought about when things were bad.

Trying to remember, telling myself that he couldn't help what he was and maybe in time he would become accustomed to ordinary domesticity and we could live a normal life."

IDLE HANDS

"Myra was a bored English girl looking for some adventure," forensic psychologist Paula Orange said. "Brady had an edge about him. Myra liked that about him, she wanted out of her dull life and into a world of edgy darkness, if you will."

Myra didn't judge Brady for being an avowed Nazi. She thought he was just going through a phase but he continued to play Richard Wagner's music full blast and storm around the house dressed up in Nazi regalia. Working himself up into a frenzy, he would then play rough sex games with Myra.

Myra found this aspect of Brady's personality to be alluring. She enjoyed dressing up in leather and black stockings, indulging whatever fantasy Brady could come up with.

"She was a sheltered young woman," Orange said. "And Brady opened up a whole new world to her. Think of it as 'Fifty Shades of Grey' with some Nazism thrown in and you have the whole relationship of Myra Hindley and Ian Brady."

The kinky sex continued and Brady gave stronger indications that he wanted to commit the perfect murder.

He wanted to harm children.

But he needed an accomplice.

"We can make the case that Myra made the jump from sadomasochistic sex to murder out of an obligation to Ian," Orange said. "It gave her a rush, to follow his lead. She needed more and more to get that same high."

The two would feed off each other sexually after which Ian would begin to plot the murders out. Who would be their victim? How would they kill them? Where would they kill them? He wrote things out in advance to the most minute detail.

"She (Myra) became desperate to fulfill his fantasies, his needs," journalist Clint Entwhistle said. "She was frightened, I suspect, of rejection by him."

So Myra didn't report him. She went along with his program.

SNAPPED

Brady had made his decision that they were going to kill someone. The night before, he took Myra to a bar on the back of his motorcycle. The two parked a little beyond the pub itself. Ian then began to intimidate Myra. He was jealous that she took a ride home from a co-worker.

"All the time we were talking," Myra recalled. "He was running a knife across his fingers. I honestly thought he was going to stab me. Then he laughed, put the knife away, told me never to accept a lift (the co-worker) again, and we drove back to the pub."

"Later as we were driving home, I dreaded what he would do when we got there, for I knew he would do something. "He raped me anally, urinated inside me and, whilst doing so, began strangling me until I nearly passed out. Then he bit me on the cheekbone, just below my right eye, until my face began to bleed. I tried to fight him off strangling me and biting me, but the more I did, the more the pressure increased. Before he left, when he'd seen the state of my face, he told me to stay off work the next day ..."

This would all take place under the roof of Myra's grandmother who was asleep when the assault took place.

"My gran almost fainted when she saw me and went to get my mother, who asked me if ' He' had done that to me. My mother disliked him intensely and kept telling me he was no good for me; she'd been telling me that since I'd met him at 18 and a half, but what girl of that age listens to her mother when she is wholly infatuated and in love? I told them what he had told me to say (she had been hit by a beer bottle during a bar fight) but I knew they didn't believe me."

THE FIRST MURDER

The following night after he beat down Myra, Brady selected his first victim.

He spotted a teenage girl walking to a dance by herself. She wore a sky blue jacket over a button-down red polka dot dress. Her white gloves and high heels turned on Ian Brady but what really arrested his attention was her face.

Cute with an air of innocence. A face that had an easy vulnerability, someone who would crack under the pressure of his whip.

Her pain and tears would be delicious, Ian thought.

Her name was Pauline Reede.

Brady gave Ian her orders and told her to pick the girl up. He would follow them on his bike.

"Ian Brady was awkward," Entwistle said. "He was not the kind of person a child would trust. There is no way anyone would have gotten into a car with him."

That is what he needed Myra for.

Myra did as he said, driving up alongside Pauline as she walked on the deserted road. The two young woman had already known each other from around the neighborhood.

"Can I give you a lift?" Myra asked.

"Oh, thank you, sure," Polly got into the small white van.

"Where are you going?"

"To the dance hall-"

"Okay," Myra said. "I just have to go to the Moors. I just lost one of my gloves. You can help me look for it. It will only take a second."

Pauline simply nodded her head. She trusted Myra.

THE KILLING FIELDS

"The Moors above Manchester were a special place for Ian Brady and Myra Hindley," Entwistle said. "They picnicked there together. They'd have sex there. It was a very, very important place to them."

It would also be the place where they would commit their first murder together.

Myra stepped off the van and directed Polly to look through some bushes. It was dark and Pauline asked if they should just look for it in the morning. Myra laughed it off and walked away, feigning as if she were looking for her gloves.

Ian Brady waited in the bushes, his mouth dry with anticipation, as he watched the sixteen-year-old Polly sift through the bushes.

Sneaking behind his victim, he slammed her across the head with a shovel.

Pauline Reede fell to the ground, stunned.

She would then be raped, tortured then murdered by the sadistic Brady.

"Brady was a sadist," Orange said. "He got off on the suffering of his young victim. The more innocent she was, the more she screamed, the more she pleaded for her life, the more he got off. It was part of the high for him. He had moved beyond the bedroom thrills with Myra and needed a bigger high. He wanted his fantasy to become reality."

Brady assaulted Pauline until she lost consciousness.

No longer able to provide him the "fun" of listening to her suffer, he took a knife to her throat and killed her.

Myra watched in silence as Ian Brady commit the brutal crime and then proceeded to bury Polly in a shallow grave.

"He led me to her body which I tried not to look at," Myra wrote. "I didn't know at the time that he was testing me at there was no need for me to be there. He told me to look at here. I'll never be able to forget what I saw. I stood and looked at the dark outline of the rocks against the horizon of the dark sky. Three people died that night. Pauline. My soul. And God. No God would have let what had happened, happen."

On the surface, however, Myra didn't seem distressed about the murder. She went to work the following Monday as if nothing happened.

"You would think if she had any conscience left she would have gone to the authorities," Orange said. "But Myra had been dehumanized by that point. The daily rapes and assaults made her numb to everything."

Still, a part of her old self remained. The disappearance of Pauline Reade sent shockwaves throughout Manchester. Myra was reading the newspaper one day and noticed a personal column written by Pauline Reade's mother.

It read " Pauline, please come home. We're heartbroken for you."

"I began to cry," Myra recalled. "Rocking myself back and forth with the paper clutched to my chest. I didn't hear his bike, nor knew that he'd come into the house. He asked me what was wrong but I couldn't answer; I couldn't stop shaking and crying, for I was devastated about what had happened to Pauline, and for her mum and dad. I really liked Mrs. Reade and used to feel sorry for her because she had problems with her nerves and always looked as though she was on the edge of a breakdown. He grabbed the paper off me and soon saw what I'd seen."

"He put the bolt on the front door in case gran came back, did the same to the back door, and began to strangle me. Before I lost consciousness, I heard him remind me of what he'd said after Pauline's murder, and that threat still stood. After the first murder, as we were driving home, he told me that if I'd shown any signs of backing out, I would have finished up in the same grave as Pauline."

MYRA'S EARLY LIFE

As one would expect, Myra grew up in an abusive home.

Her parents engaged in daily shouting matches which she watched from behind her bedroom door.

Her father would routinely beat her mother, exposing Myra to sudden violence during her formative years. He was a competitive boxer who would also engage in weekend bar brawls.

"He used to beat her a lot," Entwhistle said. "Her father was a very, very powerful influence on her life. She had a tough personality type to start with. If you combine that with a violent childhood, a childhood where she was taught how to be violent, how to be aggressive, then you end up with an unusual personality type."

Myra hated her father and saw him as a bully. He would teach her to box, often hitting her across the head when she performed the techniques incorrectly.

"My father wielded total parental control," Myra said. "I rebelled against it. Fought against it. All my life until I was old enough to free myself from it. All his attempts to control me, even the successful ones were at great cost and were the result of bitter recriminations and often a hard physical punishment."

Myra's father would give her spankings without warning, leaving her buttocks bruised.

Once when she was bullied by a little boy and came home with bruises on her face, her father locked her out of the house. He told her to either face down the bully or he was going to beat her up himself.

"I set up the street to meet my persecutor," Myra recalled. "I quickly concentrated on whatDad had told me and showed me. As Kenny's hand came up, I shot up my left hand, fist bunched towards his head. As I predicted, both hands went up to protect his face and I lifted my right hand and slammed it into his tummy, hitting him hard. With a gasp, Kenny Holden's knees crumbled and before he could recover I slammed my left fist into the side of his head. Kenny was so heavily shocked he sat down heavily on the floor and burst into tears. I stood looking down at him triumphantly."

Myra saw a lot of her father in Ian Brady. Aggressive. Ultra-violent.

"Myra did what we call in psychology, 'transference,'" Orange said. "She saw in Ian what she saw in her father. She never got her daddy's love. So in her mind, she saw Ian as Daddy. She wanted Daddy's love and would do whatever Ian wanted. That was part of her cycle.

Transferring a deep need for her father's love onto Ian. There is the strong possibility that had Myra never hooked up with Ian she would have never become a murderer. But the two of them together? Horrific results."

"The bringing together of Myra Hindley and Ian Brady," Entwhistle said. "Unleashed an appalling set of criminal acts."

POLLY IS STILL MISSING

The disappearance of Polly Reede sent the town of Manchester on edge. Things like that simply didn't happen there.

"The fact that children were being abducted and killed," Entwhistle said. "Was incomprehensible to the ordinary man and woman in the street."

Myra would soon find out that Ian's sexual fantasies were not limited to teenaged girls.

He wanted boys too.

Myra would again be a willing accomplice in procuring Ian's second victim. This time, it would be twelve-year-old John Killbride. Myra would befriend the young boy before bringing him to the Moors where he would be sexually assaulted by Brady and later killed.

"I had a terrible feeling something had happened to him," John Killbridge's mother recalled when her son didn't come home from school. "Because he wasn't the kind of boy who would leave home for any reason. He was quite happy and very pleasant, always singing and whistling and I just couldn't see him going anywhere with anyone. Unless it was in an innocent way, somebody wanting to do a job with him or something like that. He'd be enticed into a car that way."

Ian would take photos of the body and burial site. This would become part of their ritual, their ceremony. They would perform the murder then take photographs as if to mark the moment. Then they would return to the scene of the crime days after with their dog "Puppet" in tow. They would take more pictures and relive what took place only days earlier.

"He stopped me as I was walking (to take a picture)," Myra recalled. "And said to turnaround. Moved me about a bit. Told me to kneel down and look at 'Puppet' whose head was showing when he was still wrapped inside my coat. I now know, and knew quite soon afterward, that he photographed me virtually kneeling on John Killbride's grave."

AN INSATIABLE HUNGER

Four months had elapsed between the Pauline and John Killbride murders. But now Ian could not wait long. He ordered Myra to deliver another victim to the isolated Moors.

His name was Keith Bennett. An exuberant, trusting boy, Keith looked like the proverbial nerd with a gap-toothed smile and professorial eyeglasses.

"Keith was a cheeky little lad," Entwhistle said. "He liked to go out and have fun."

Trusting that Myra was taking him some place fun, the young Keith was ambushed by Brady who wrapped a cord around his neck.

Myra did her usual best to remain detached while the horrific attack took place.

"I hadn't wanted this to happen," Myra recalled. "I was tense and terrified. I tried to concentrate my mind miles away from where I was. Finally, after roughly what I think was a half an hour by which time dusk began to descend. I heard him whistle or call. When I stood up, he was waving me back down to the stream bed. Virtually nothing was said as we made our way back except for him saying the spade was hampering him and he'd have to hide it, which he did."

The twelve-year-old Keith, whose entire family was waiting for him at his grandmother's house, never showed up.

His entire family would be traumatized for life.

"I am a mother," Keith's mother, Winnie Johnson said. "It was my first lad and I've got to find him no matter what."

Keith Bennett's body was never found.

"I have nightmares," Johnson said. "I jump in my sleep. It's getting to me now. Because I just can't get him back."

Meanwhile, Myra and Ian would once again take mementos of their time together, taking photos of themselves along the Moors on Keith's fresh grave. Days later, the two would go to St. James Church for midnight mass.

"I retained a warm religious glow," Myra said. "And came out feeling warmed. Not so Ian who took a long swill of whiskey and went to the grave where he casually urinated."

RITUALS

The photos of their time together became an obsession for Ian Brady. He had an automatic camera where he would set the timer and pose for photographs with Myra. In a few of them, they would pose on top of the fresh graves with Ian playfully choking Myra.

"Myra and Ian would often return to the scenes of their crimes," Orange said. "They would take photos of themselves there and relive the thrill of committing the murders."

Over time, however, the photos would not be enough stimulation. They needed something better. Something more visceral.

Sounds.

Ian Brady decided he would record the audio of their next victim being tortured.

That next victim would be ten-year-old Leslie Ann Downey. Myra would befriend and abduct her from the county fairgrounds.

"They would take her back to their home," Entwistle said. "Where he photographed her and recorded her being tortured."

Ian Brady would listen to the audio tape over and over again, closing his eyes and remembering the horrific acts he committed.

Is is the murder of Leslie that Myra would refuse to talk about in interviews.

"There's a tape that isn't what people think it is," Myra said, trying to downplay her own sadism evident in the tapes. "But it's bad. I just hurt so much to think that I've been such a cruel bastard."

THE RUSH OF KILLING

Like a drug addict needing a bigger hit to get high, Brady needed more and more of a thrill for his next murder. He started to get sloppy whereas before his attacks were meticulously planned out.

His next victim would be Edward Evans.

"Edwards was sixteen, seventeen years old," Entwhistle said. "And he picked him up in a pub in Manchester."

This would be the first time Ian acted in tandem with Myra to obtain the victim. They enticed the young man to come over to their home and there were witnesses in the pub.

The couple also invited Myra's brother in law, Dave Smith to watch the carnage.

"Smith had no idea what was going on," Entwhistle said. "He walked into it totally cold, totally unaware and soon found out that he was involved in the most horrific scene with blood all over the place. A man's head being smashed in."

Smith was appalled, then called the police and told them of the killing.

Police arrived on scene within minutes. They discovered the mauled body of Edwards in a tub. Both Ian and Myra would be arrested.

"It is inexplicable as to why the couple would allow Dave Smith to witness the murder," Orange said. "A part of me thinks that it was part of increasing the thrill. The desire to share what they felt was a special moment with someone else."

A CHILLING DISCOVERY

Investigators would then scour the home, finding one unusual clue that would reveal the goings on of the couple now known in the papers as the Moors Murderers.

They found a left over luggage ticket.

The police would go to the central train station and matched the ticket with a suitcase. Inside, the found something they would never forget.

"They kept trophies in suitcases," Entwhistle said. "In there, of course, was the tape recording of Leslie Ann Downey and that proved what they'd done."

The police would play back the tapes. It churned their stomach to hear the tearful cries of Leslie Ann Downey plead for her life.

"You need to do what he says," Hindley screamed at the little girl. "I told you to shut your face!"

"I want to go home," the little girl pleaded.

"Quiet! Do you not speak English?"

The tape would be played for the jurors at the trial of the couple.

According to witnesses, you could hear a pin drop when they played the tape in court.

"Afterward there was a long, stony silence," Entwhistle said. "As people reflected on what they just heard."

DENIAL

Myra would maintain her own innocence of the murders and repeatedly state that she never witnessed any of the killings herself.

"My solicitor (defense attorney) told me they'd found the body of a child," Myra said. "Identified as Lesley Ann Downey, did I know anything about it? And I said 'No.' A week after that, I'm not sure, they found John Killbride's body and they charged me with, I think it was the murder of John Killbride. Yes, it was. They set me down behind a table and behind it was a large poster of John Killbride. 'Will you just identify these pictures or these photos and tell us if you seen them before.' I'd say, yes, and then they turned over the picture to another photo of the unearthed body of John Killbride."

The picture, Myra would state, made her cry.

LETTERS TO MOMMA

Myra would write her mother numerous letters before her trial. She would order her mother to destroy the letters after she read them but her mother thought otherwise. She would also tell her mother to keep the photographs of her and Ian to herself.

"Don't believe what they're saying about us," Myra wrote. "It is all lies."

But the mothers of all the victims didn't see it that way.

In court, they all had an opportunity to confront Myra.

"The worst part was being confronted by Mrs. West in the witness box," Myra recalled. "And I was looking at her as she was giving evidence and she saw me looking at her and she screamed across at me. 'How can you look at me?' And she called me every name under the sun."

It is at this point that Myra stated that she began to fully realize the gravity of her crimes.

"It suddenly hit me just what I'd done and I think he (Ian) sensed this," Myra said. "We were sitting next to each other and he just put his hand on my arm and squeezed my arm. And I turned around and looked at him, and he was telling me with his eyes to keep quiet."

The jury would find them guilty and in May of 1966 both would be sentenced to life in prison.

STANDING BY HER MAN

Myra refused to testify against Ian. There were some legal experts at the time who believed that if she gave evidence against Brady she would have walked free. But she didn't. She elected to take the punishment along with him.

Instead, she accepted her sentencing and continued to write her mother.

"Dear Mum," Myra wrote. "I knew that I would have to go to prison for some time for 'harboring'. But I didn't think it would be for this long. Ian is in prison, in the special wing. Poor thing, he sews mailbags during the day. He says it helps to pass the time quicker than expected. Will you do one thing for me, ma'am? Take out a policy on me or for me, for a half gram a week. I can't even begin to think of the future. It will be something to fall back on."

"Ian has got a little mouse in his cell. He feeds it crumbs and sits in bed watching it nibble them. The other night, he left it half a chip, thinking it wouldn't touch it but when he woke up the next morning it had disappeared."

Over the next three years, Myra would bombard her mother with requests for the photographs of her and Ian together. She said she did this at the behest of Ian who wanted both the slides and photographs desperately. Myra's mother eventually relented by was sure to allow the police copies of the negatives.

"Ian wanted those pictures back so bad because it reminded him of the events," Orange said. "That is the sort of thing we've come to expect from certain types of serial killers. They want to relive the moment in their fantasy. They'll take mementos, pictures, different elements of their crime in order so they can relive it in their minds. The pictures of Myra holding their dog on those burial sites were of paramount importance to Ian."

Myra would die in prison in 2002 of respiratory failure. Her ashes would be scattered over the Moors, a place that she loved so much.

"Was Myra Hindley sick or was she evil?" Entwhistle asked. "She had a violent father. She met a sexually sadistic man who desperately wanted to be a serial killer. All those things came together and made her carry out some evil, appalling crimes."

Ian Brady remains alive, living out his years under suicide watch in a psychiatric facility where he has repeatedly stated that he will kill himself if given the chance.